DHAKA

From Mughal Outpost to Metropolis

DHAKA

From Mughal Outpost to Metropolis

Golam Rabbani

 The University Press Limited

The University Press Limited
Red Crescent House
61 Motijheel Commercial Area
G.P.O. Box 2611
Dhaka 1000
Bangladesh

Fax: (88 02) 9565443
E-mail: upl@bangla.net, upl@bttb.net.bd
website: www.uplbooks.com

Third Impression 2006
Second Impression 2000
First Published 1997

Concept, Photography, and Design: GOLAM RABBANI
Text: GOLAM RABBANI AND NAZIM UDDIN AHMED
Text Editor: NIAZ ZAMAN
Consulting Editor: L. LEWINTER SUSKIND

Photo Legends

ISBN 984 05 1374 5

Front cover: Traffic jam in a Dhaka street
Back cover: Curzon Hall, Dhaka University
Page 2: Sunset on Buriganga river
Page 5: Chawk Bazar in old city
Page 6: Part of the Interior of the City of Dacca:
A Sketch by Charles D'Oyly, 1814
Page 7: *Minar* of Lalbagh Mosque
Page 8: Mural on Osmani Memorial Hall
Page 12: Wall decoration on Qassabtuli Mosque
Page 16: Remains of *Baro Katra.*

Published by Mohiuddin Ahmed, The University Press
Limited, Dhaka and printed at the Akota Offset Press,
119 Fokirapool, Dhaka, Bangladesh.

Dedicated to many generations of
Dhakaiyas who lived, prospered, and
died in this part of Bengal

Drawn by C.D'Oyly Esq.

PART of the INTERIOR of the CITY of DACCA.

Inscribed with profound Respect to his Highness Nusrut Jung Nabob of Dacca.

Engraved by G.Cooke & R.Landseer Engraver to the King E.S.A.

Published 4 June 1824 by R.Landseer 33 Foley Street London.

Contents

Foreword

During my school years, almost forty years ago, when my parents paid a short visit to Dhaka, they took me with them and that was my first sojourn to Dhaka. We arrived at the old Fulbaria Railway Station near Gulistan, hired a horse-driven cart called *tikka gari,* and went to a small boarding-house in the old town, the location I cannot remember now.

That was my first introduction to anything called a town or city, and everything seemed so unfamiliar and strange to me that I felt like returning home the very next day. However, as time went by, many things changed for me and when I came back to Dhaka again several years later as a student of medicine, the feeling was still not very comfortable but definitely less uncomfortable. This time my feeling was softening and I started liking the city as deeply as I had once hated it before.

Sometime later, in the early 1960s, when I was developing a fascination for photography, I was able to borrow a fixed focus roll film camera and took some pictures of buildings. Same size black and white prints from 120 negatives, popularly known as B2 size, was the standard of photography in those days. When I saw the prints I was deeply moved and fascinated, not because the prints were great but because I could prove to others that I could do this. Since then I have been enjoying immense pleasure in taking photographs and writing about the city I have come to love during the three decades of uninterrupted living in this great metropolis. Although I am neither a historian nor a professional photographer, I have developed a strong interest in these two complementary disciplines, of course as a hobbyist, and these have become my important pastimes for many years. One of my senior American friends and a diplomat who knew my work once remarked that "I have been wasting my time in medicine."

During the last ten years or so, I have been photographing Dhaka city and have accumulated thousands of pictures on different aspects of the city taken with different types of cameras under different conditions of light, climate, and perspectives.

The job of selecting photographs for this volume has been both enjoyable and immensely difficult. For each picture that has been selected there are many alternatives and varieties of pictures, each of them too good to be rejected. Because there are numerous ways in which a landscape, a girl, or a flower can be photographed, and no particular way is necessarily the best way.

Dhaka is an interesting city and has the common characteristics of the big cities of the developing world. The city is fast changing, traditional ways of life are giving ways to modern styles in all aspects of life. In the waves of the so-called modernism, many traditional elements and values, that are unique to this city, will eventually be swept away without leaving a record. In today's Dhaka, the traditional conch shell cutters of Shankhari Bazar have almost disappeared, the numbers of old masters of gold and silver jewellers in Tanti Bazar have declined, and the colourful rickshaws of Dhaka streets would soon be obsolete. The aim of this volume is to record some of these vanishing world so that the future readers can trace the linkage to our lost heritage.

Every city big or small, rich or poor, has its own story to tell. Every major city of the world has a dark side, be it violence, poverty, unemployment, natural calamity, or menace. Dhaka has its misery and poverty too. But above all, it has a remarkable, amorphous quality of life, the coherence of living together, often with a touch of oblivion.

Dhaka, March 1997   *Golam Rabbani*

ACKNOWLEDGEMENTS

It took me more than five years to prepare the materials of this book. During this period I came across many individuals who directly or indirectly helped me at various stages of my work. I am indebted to Sushila Zaitlyn and Jonathan for their continuous encouragement and support. I must thank Josephine Sack for her day-to-day advice and criticism; thanks also to her husband Bradley Sack for his support. Acknowledgments are also due to Moslem Ali, Mohammad Mohsin, and Akmam Afroz of National Museum for helping me take photographs of the museum specimens. Special thanks to Fazlul Hassan Yusuf for continuously boosting my morale and confidence and also to Michael Bennish for practical support. Thanks also go to A. K. M. Siddique for his positive encouragement; and Mahabubul Hoque, and Ekram Hossain for their secretarial help.

I offer special appreciation to Mrs. Lewinter Suskind, Lousiana State University; Mohiuddin Ahmed, Director General, Radio Bangladesh; S. I. Khan, Head, ICDDR,B Library; and Rumana Siddique, Dhaka University for their editorial help. Thanks also to A. M. Saadullah and Masiuddin Shaker for their special help with designing and editing respectively. I must thank Professor Niaz Zaman for her final revision of the texts. Finally, I must thank Mohiuddin Ahmed, Managing Director of The University Press Limited and BRAC Printers for their active support with the production of this book.

PHOTOGRAPHIC NOTE

For the pictures of this volume I have used several models of large, medium, and 35 mm format cameras. For the aerial shots, cityscapes, and the architectural subjects I have extensively used 4x5 view cameras with a variety of lenses. For other shots I have used either a medium format (6x6, 6x7 or 6x9) or a 35 mm SLR, each with a variety of lenses of different focal lengths. Fujichrome professional film for all formats was my major brand for most application, although I have used Kodak Ektachrome film in some instances. I have always used a Sekonic handheld light meter for determining exposures before shooting. The films were processed mostly locally and some were done in USA, Singapore, and Australia.

Preface

Dhaka from the sky is a photographer's dream. I realised this the day I was shooting an aerial view from atop a building high above the Malibagh Bazar. What might have been the entire population of the world jostled along the narrow streets below, weaving in and out of shops, haggling at tiny stalls with voices loud enough to carry even to my great height. The merchandise looked like a child's miniatures: tiny pots and pans, fabrics for saris, dried fish, green chilies, and tiny baskets of colourful fruits.

A railway track passed through the middle of the Bazar, grocery baskets littering what appeared to be its abandoned lines. The hissing noise of an approaching train was both startling and frightening. My apprehension was that the train would cause a fatal disaster. To my surprise, nothing of the sort happened. The train rushed through at break-neck speed, its final destination far more important than the dense humanity it was cutting through. The crowds opened up to let the train through and then closed up again. The routine of the Bazar resumed as if the train had been no more than a passing thought, barely touching consciousness.

The Malibagh Bazar is, however, more than a picturesque dot in a picturesque country. It stands as a symbol of survival, an example of how far desperate the people will go, indeed, must go, to fight against succumbing to poverty. In another place, another economic world, setting up shops in the shadow of a dangerous railway line would be unthinkable. But, where roads and railway lines are the only accessible places, Bazars spring up, convenient to shoppers and vendors alike. The train becomes a slight inconvenience, disrupting a few moments of business each day.

Besides the Bazars, rickshaws form the most integral part of the city life in Dhaka. Everyday, more than a hundred thousand rickshaws wend through the streets of Dhaka, their tinkling bells blending in the general cacophony, their gaily decorated hoods and brightly painted boards constituting a moving art gallery. In a world that is moving towards faster - but perhaps more environmentally unsound means of transportation - the rickshaws meet approximately sixty per cent of all transportation needs and provide employment to an estimated two hundred fifty thousand urban poor.

Often considered a nuisance by the city planners, the rickshaw is a blessing for the passenger it carries. For a pittance, it will go anywhere, anytime, in the hot sun, in drenching rain, through back alleys, often rubbing shoulder with giant trucks and and buses, on jammed streets.

With trains whistling through its Bazars, rickshaws weaving through its thoroughfares, bamboo and polythene shanties mocking its luxury hotels, Dhaka is a city of incongruities and anachronisms. It is a city that has barely stepped out of its nineteenth century past into a present, bombarded with the latest technological advancements.

Provincial capital of the Mughals, factory town to the East India Company, university town after the annulment of the Bengal partition, second capital after the creation of Pakistan, centre of political movements, Dhaka was catapulted to the problematic prominence of a capital city after the birth of Bangladesh. Forced to keep pace with the demands of a capital, Dhaka expanded both in terms of its size and population.

The city's rapid and often unplanned urbanisation during the last two decades has changed its appearance. Splendid high-rise buildings, an evidence of a real-estate boom, have sprung up all over the city, catering to the needs of city-dwellers, foreign diplomats, and international consultants. Improved travel facilities, better communication links, and the ubiquitous dish antennas have brought the sleepy *mofussil* (rural) town closer to becoming a megalopolis.

The legacy of Dhaka's glorious past blends with present realities, in rich, if at times, incongruous, contrasts. This book is an attempt to capture in photographs, some of the of this city at once old and new.

A Brief History of Dhaka

Dhaka, the capital city of Bangladesh, sprawls gracefully on the northern bank of the river Buriganga, a silent witness of the vicissitudes of history.

Though little is known of the pre-Mughal past of Dhaka, its tombs and shrine inscriptions, dating to the fourteenth and fifteenth centuries, testify to the early settlement of the area.

The earliest monuments of Dhaka are the *dargahs, khankahs,* tombs, and mosques of Arab saints and missionaries who preached Islam in the Dhaka region. Among the shrines are that of Shah Ali Baghdadi who died in 1498 and was buried in Mirpur. Devotees still flock to his tomb.

The stone inscriptions belong to the reign of the independent Sultan Nasiruddin Mahmood Shah (1435-1459). The first one, fixed over the entrance of an old pre-Mughal mosque at Narinda, dated 861 Hijri/1457 AD, is curiously inscribed in Persian as well as in Arabic. The original structure of the mosque, measuring ten feet six inches square, although extensively renovated, still retains some of its old features including the drumless single dome, curved cornice, octagonal corner towers, and portions of the walls. The inscription notes that the mosque was commissioned by Musammat Bakht Binat, daughter of Marhamat.

The second inscription, now preserved in the National Museum at Dhaka, was fixed on the wall of an old mosque in Naswalla Galli, located near the Central Jail. The inscription records that a gate was strengthened and built during the reign of Sultan Nasiruddin Abul Muzaffar Mahmud Shah on 20th Sha'ban, 863 Hijri, that is 25th June, 1459 by a person bearing the title of Khan-i-Jahan.

Islam Khan Chisti, the first Mughal Viceroy of Bengal, arrived in Dhaka approximately in 1608-1610, during the reign of the Mughal Emperor Jahangir in Delhi.

Islam Khan established a fortified post in Dhaka, called it Jahangir Nagar, and declared it the capital of the Bengal Subah or province. The Mughals remained in control for one hundred fifty-three years, until 1763, when the British officially took over the city by purchasing the Diwani (revenue administration) of Bengal, Bihar, and Orissa provinces.

During the Mughal reign, Dhaka enjoyed the status of a provincial capital and experienced phenomenal commercial growth. The Mughals built elegant forts, magnificent mosques, tombs, *katras* (houses), and bridges. These include the Lalbagh Fort, Boro Katra, Chotto Katra, Hussaini Dalan, Pari Bibi's Tomb, Tongi Bridge, Dulai Bridge, and Pagla Bridge. Trade, commerce, and industry flourished.

The city's phenomenal growth from an insignificant position of a military outpost of the far-flung Mughal Empire to the position of a provincial capital earned it the nickname of 'Queen of the cities in Eastern India'.

The flourishing trade, commerce, and cotton textile industries of Dhaka during the Mughal period attracted European traders to settle and establish their factories there. European companies, particularly the Portuguese, Dutch, English, and French, as well as East Asians, Armenians, Persians, and Arabs started coming in large numbers from the late 17th century. This melange of cultures, added to the existing one, contributed significantly to the city's development as a cultural and multinational trading centre. A wide range of goods left the ports of Dhaka during this time, including fine cotton muslin, products from shells, bamboo, metal, and, gold and silver jewellery. Agricultural products including unrefined sugar, mustard seeds, honey, ghee (melted butter), cheese, betel nut, oil, pulses, ginger, and other spices also added to the revenue collected as export duties at Dhaka's river ports.

In 1717, the capital of Bengal was shifted from Dhaka to Murshidabad by Nawab Murshid Kuli Khan, the Diwan (chief revenue administrator) of Bengal, initiating a downward trend in the status and ability of Dhaka. In the 1740s, Dhaka's economy was adversely affected by the Marathas from south India who invaded Bengal, marauding and plundering. The immediate effect of the Maratha atrocities was to exacerbate the problems in Dhaka and further weaken Bengal. The final, shattering blow to Bengal autonomy, however, was delivered at the battle of Plassey in 1757, when Nawab Sirajuddaulla, the young Nawab of Bengal, Bihar, and Orissa, was defeated. The British East India Company became the supreme executive authority in Bengal, including, of course, Dhaka.

The acquisition of Diwani gave the British East India Company an extraordinarily advantageous position. From that time, it held a monopoly over the other European companies in all matters of trade and administration. It also dealt a critical blow to Dhaka's cotton industry when the invention of mechanised textile manufacturing in England not only reduced British dependence on foreign textiles but also made it look for markets. To achieve this, the British East India Company began restricting the trading rights of other European companies in Dhaka and prohibiting local weavers from selling their products to non-British companies. As a result, by 1787, the production of cotton textiles had dropped precipitously and most weavers had gone out of business.

During the early 18th century, the social structure of Dhaka was characterised by culturally identifiable classes that were similar to the feudal social system of England in the middle ages. Between the top British East India Company executives at one end of the hierarchy and the landless peasants or the weavers on the other, were the nobility, such as *lakherajdar, faujdar, banias, mutsuddis, gomostha, paikar, dalal, kayal, talukdar, tahsildar, paiks,* and *peadas* which were the Indian versions of English barons, earls, dukes, and, knights. This native hierarchy was protected and pampered for its own political ends by the British East India Company.

One of the most important positions held by the nobility was that of Naib-Nazim (City Administrator). The first Naib-Nazim of Dhaka to be selected by the Company was Jasarat Khan (1757-1760). He was given the title of Nawab and given the authority to rule locally as an agent of the Company. He and his family lived in an elegantly built palace called Nimtali Kuthi which stood near the site of the old National Museum building and the present Asiatic Society.

The one family that was able to attain political, economic, and social power was the family of Khawja Alimullah who originally came from Kashmir in north India in the early 18th century in search of better life in Dhaka. Starting off as a petty trader, he amassed wealth to secure vast *zamindaris* in Dhaka, Mymensingh, Faridpur, Barisal, Tripura, and Chittagong. His annual income was said to be over one million rupees. Because of the family's close association with the British colonial rulers, they enjoyed the highest administrative privileges; and both Khawja Abdul Gani (1813 -1896) and his son Khawja Ahsanullah (1846 -1901) received the hereditary title of Nawab, a symbol of direct British patronage. They were popularly known as the Nawabs of Dhaka.

The Nawab family used its influence in the development of public welfare systems in the city. It helped establish a water supply pipe-line in Dhaka in 1878 and electricity in 1901. In the 1860s '70s, Nawab Khawja Abdul Gani and Nawab Khawja Ahsanullah served as municipal commissioners, developing the race-course Maidan, Motijheel, and the Shahbagh areas. Nawab Ahsanullah also established Dhaka Survey School, later turned into Ahsanullah Engineering College and, finally, into today's Bangladesh University of Engineering and Technology. During the 19th century, they also provided the necessary leadership to the Bengali Muslim movement which led to the establishment of All India Muslim League in 1905 and the creation of an independent Muslim state, Pakistan, in 1947.

While its power had been declining since the late 19th century, the abolition of the *zamindari* system in 1951 dealt the final blow to the power of the Nawab family. The magnificent Nawab palace, Ahsan Manzil, was converted into a museum in 1993.

In 1854, the British established the Bengal Presidency to govern the regions of Bengal, Bihar, Orissa, and Assam. Dhaka had, of course, lost the status of a capital city in 1717 when the capital was transferred to Mursidabad. However, on October 16, 1905, after almost two centuries of political upheaval and turmoil under the British colonial rule, the city regained the capital status of Bengal once again, when a new province of Bengal and Assam was created by Lord Curzon with Dhaka as its capital. The establishment of the capital at Dhaka resulted in a phenomenal expansion of activity in the city. Government houses, office buildings, assembly halls, and residential areas were established. In 1911, however, the partition of Bengal was annulled. At about the same time, the administrative centre of Bengal was transferred from Calcutta to Delhi.

Dhaka did not become a provincial capital again until 1947 when the British finally left India after nearly two centuries of colonial rule and the two independent nations, India and Pakistan, came into being. Dhaka became the provincial capital of East Pakistan. The area in Dhaka which is known today as Sher-e-Bangla Nagar was designed and developed as a second capital of independent Pakistan.

In 1971, after a long-standing economic, cultural, and political friction between the eastern and western provinces of Pakistan, a war of liberation broke out. At its end, the eastern province of Pakistan had become the independent sovereign state of Bangladesh and Dhaka had, once again, become a capital city.

2

Dhaka : From Mughal Outpost to Modern Megalopolis

Dhaka's growth from a small pre-Mughal town to a megalopolis, boasting more than eight million people is a collage of contributions by its own indigenous inhabitants and many invaders, Mughal, Afghan, English, Armenian, Portuguese, Greek, French, or Arab, who made it their home, temporary or permanent. Though the importance of Dhaka begins with the invasion of Islam Khan, there existed a pre-Mughal Dhaka in the area between the Buriganga river and one of its tributaries called *Dolai khal*. The arrival of the Mughals extended this area, so that in 1640, when Sebastian Manrique visited Dhaka, the city had extended to Hazaribagh and Maneswar in the west and Narinda in the east.

Today Dhaka stretches from Postagola in the south to Tongi in the north - a line of growth that followed the Mughal pattern.

The Mughals

Baharistan-i-ghaibi, an account written by Mirza Nathan, Admiral of the Mughal fleet who accompanied Islam Khan, records in astonishing detail, the conditions of Dhaka and its adjacent areas. Mirza Nathan described Dhaka as standing on the river Dulai. Describing his journey to the Fort of Islam Khan, Mirza Nathan noted that there stood a *pakur* tree midway between the old and the new city, and also midway between his house and the residence of Islam Khan. The site of this old fort has been identified with the Central Jail area. The site where the *pakur* tree stood as a landmark during Mirza Nathan's time has been identified with the area known as Pakurtali, currently occupied by the Salimullah Medical College and Hospital (former Mitford Hospital).

The present old city is divided into unequal halves at the Malitola - Tantibazar corner where an artificial canal of the Buriganga, east of Pakurtali, joins the Dulai creek. The artificial canal most probably was dug at Islam Khan's initiative to serve as a moat to the new settlement. The old city, enclosed within the two branches of the Dulai rivulet, was believed to have been originally occupied by the *tantis* (weavers) and *shankharis* (conch shell cutters), who lent their names to their localities. Many areas still carry Hindu names suggesting the pre-Mughal origin of the city. These areas include Laksmi Bazar, Sutrapur, Jaluanagar, Banianagar, Goalnagar, Chutarnagar, Kamarnagar, Potuatuli, Kumartuli etc. The new city grew up across the west bank of the moat during the Mughal period. Mughaltuli in this locality was probably named during the same period.

Around the old fort (inside the present Central Jail) there were Badshahi Bazar (now Chawk Bazar), Peel Khana, or the site of royal elephant stable, Mahut-tuli (quarters for the elephant keepers) and so on. The area of present Diwan Bazar was a posh area set apart for officials of distinction like ministers, diwans and secretaries. The sparsely built Ramna area with elegant mansions and bungalows was also laid out with an attractive royal garden, known as *Bagh-i-Badshahi* near the present old High Court building, where Islam Khan was temporarily buried after his tragic death in 1613.

Sebastian Manrique, visiting Dhaka in 1640, noted that "the city extended over a league and a half (a league = 3.5 miles) from Manaxor (Maneswar) at one end and up to (Narinda) and Fulgari (Phulbaria) at the other which rounded off the city suitably." His statement shows that, since the days of Islam Khan, the city expanded, virtually doubled its size to the west.

During the Mughal Prince Shah Shuja's vice-royalty (1639-1660), two important monuments were built in Dhaka: the *Boro Katra* (1644), and the *Choto Katra* (1663) near Chawk Bazar overlooking the Buriganga river and the great Idgah (1640) along Satmasjid Road. *Boro Katra*, built by Mir Abul Qasim, the deputy, was meant to be the palace of Shah Shuja but it is said that the prince did not like the building and therefore, endowed it to its builder, Mir Abul Qasim. In 1649, a singledomed mosque with three *mihrabs* was erected near Chawk Bazar by a Mughal officer, named Muhammad Beg. Another *katra* or caravanserai was built in 1660 near the Chawk by the Daroga (Chief of Police) of the royal fleet, Muhammad Muqim. The building does not exist at present but the site is still known as Muqim *Katra*.

Mir Jumla, who was the Mughal Viceroy from 1659 to 1663, erected a number of important buildings in Dhaka. To protect the capital against the recurrent raids of the Mughs and the Portuguese buccaneers, he built many river forts and bridges along the water routes to the capital, including Tongi Bridge (now collapsed), and the three-arched bridge over the Pagla creek.

Nawab Shaista Khan

Nawab Shaista Khan, son of Asaf Khan, the Prime Minister of the Mughal Emperor, was unquestionably the greatest of the Mughal Viceroys in Bengal. During his rule of nearly a quarter century, from 1664 to 1678 and from 1679 to 1688, he reversed the chaotic condition and indiscipline in the administration following Shah Shuja's departure from Bengal. Peace and tranquillity in the province prevailed during his twenty-two years of viceroyalty. He built a large number of magnificent edifices in Dhaka such as the Sat Gombuj Masjid, *Choto Katra*, Chawk Masjid, the unfinished Lalbagh Fort. He introduced a distinctive architectural style which, later came to be known as the 'Shaista Khani' style.

Prince Muhammad Azam, the pleasure-loving second son of Emperor Aurangzeb was the viceroy of Bengal for a brief period of about sixteen months from July 1678 to October 1679. During his short tenure of office he probably began the construction of the Lalbagh Fort, overlooking the Buriganga river, but left it unfinished. It appears from the writings of contemporary western travelers that Dhaka at that time extended from Demra on the east to Mirpur on the west, and from Buriganga on the south to Tongi on the north.

Prince Muhammad Azimuddin (later Azimush Shan), the grandson of Aurangzeb continued as the Governor of Bengal till 1712. He built a new palace along the Buriganga river at Posta area, southeast of Lalbagh Fort. A large part of the palace-cum-residence of the prince, as noted by James Taylor, was engulfed by the river, leaving only a small portion to survive during his time. Some scholars think that the present Azimpur locality was named after the prince.

The Dutch

Being attracted by the agrarian wealth of the Indian subcontinent, tradesmen from different European nations started arriving in this region as early as the 15th century. In 1498, the Dutch fleet of Vasco da Gama anchored at the west coast of India, near Goa which gradually developed into a prolific Dutch commercial centre. The Dutch moved eastward later, and, by 1666, the United East India Company of Netherlands built a factory on the bank of the Buriganga river at Dhaka, on a site now occupied by the Mitford Medical College and Hospital. In 1781, the factory was surrendered to the British East India Company who seized all their properties in Dhaka including a garden and mansion at Tejgaon .

The French

The French settlers in Dhaka were mainly concentrated around the present site of Farashganj - the word *farashi* being Bengali for French. Wealthy French traders also settled in scattered groups in Tejgaon. A French factory was established in Islampur on the river bank in 1740 at the site now occupied by Ahsan Manzil.

The Armenians

Armenians also established a colony in Dhaka and took a leading role in the jute trade. In the 19th century they had a flourishing trade in textiles, salt, and betelnut. Some Armenians even acquired *zamindaris* and became landlords. At Tejgaon there are some old Armenian graves, dated to the 18th century within the Roman Catholic church premises. An elegant Armenian church and cemetery still exist in the Armanitola area of the old city.

The Greeks

A Greek colony was founded in the 18th century by the descendants of Alexis Argyree, the leader of the Greek settlers in Calcutta. Their first church in Dhaka was erected in 1821. The Greek community in Dhaka was chiefly engaged in the jute and salt trades. The remnant of the old Greek trading community is still traceable in Narayanganj; the most prominent being the Rally Brothers. An elegant Greek memorial is located within the Dhaka University's Teacher Student Centre. It is a small, square, dainty little building with fluted Doric columns carrying atop a triangular pediment containing a Greek inscription recording, "In memory of Philipa and Prosilebu'. There are nine blackstone grave epitaphs in Greek and five in English within the building dating between 1800 and 1843.

The British

The British East India Company's securing the Diwani of Bengal, Bihar, and Orissa marked the beginning of the British administration in Dhaka. Theoretically, the administration of the state was divided into Diwani (authority for collecting revenues), administration of civil justice, and Nizamat (power of commanding troops and dispensing criminal justice). The grant of the Diwani to the Company and the retention of Nizamat by the Nawab introduced a dual system of administration in the province. The greatest evil of this system was that the Company was vested with absolute power to collect revenue from the land but without the responsibility of maintaining law and order. As a consequence, the Company became an exploiting machine while the Nawab, stripped of the power of revenue collection, became a titular administrator.

Bishop Heber who visited Dhaka in 1824 testified to the decay of the city. From 1830 onwards this trend was reversed with new expansion and development. Islampur, Tanti Bazar, Goalnagar, and Rai Saheb Bazar which were low-lying areas subject to flooding, were gradually filled in and the present court building and the erstwhile State Bank building (now demolished to house the present Jagannath University College) were established. The Wari area, originally a *Khas* land, was leased out in 1835 for rehabilitation, and became the habitat of the middle class gentry of the town. During this period, the Dhaka Municipality, the Dhaka District Board, and the foundation of the Dhaka Government School and College, were laid at the initiatives of Mr. Walters, the District Magistrate, Dr. James Taylor, Surgeon, and Mr. Grant, the local Magistrate.

The Nawabs of Dhaka

With the last Naib Nazim - Ghaziuddin Haider's death in 1843, the line of the Mughal Nawabs came to an end. But a new line of titular Nawab families, unconnected with the old rulers of the province, rose to prominence in Dhaka, the courtesy title of Nawab being conferred by the British Government in recognition of their munificence and public service. They played an active role in the freedom movement of the Muslims in the subcontinent, the Muslim League being founded in Dhaka on the initiative of Khwaja Abdul Hakim and Maulvi Abdullah who came to Bengal from Kashmir in 1739 and started trading in leather goods. They eventually acquired extensive land properties in Dhaka, Sylhet, Bakergonj, Comilla, and Mymensingh districts. Maulvi Abdullah's grandson, Khwaja Alimullah, purchased the French Factory in 1838, and on that site, his son Abdul Ghani erected the imposing Ahsan Manzil, naming it after his son Ahsanullah Bahadur.

The Partition of Bengal

In 1904, the Viceroy, Lord Curzon came to Dhaka and stayed as the royal guest of Nawab Salimullah at Ahsan Manzil. In February 1904 he laid the foundation of the Curzon Hall, originally meant to be a townhall, and announced that the site would soon be developed into a new town. The scheme finally adopted by Lord Curzon was to unite Assam and Chittagong with fifteen districts of Bengal to form the new province of East Bengal and Assam with its capital at Dhaka. Its population, predominantly Muslim, was at that time thirty-one million.

In 1911, the British Government annulled Curzon's partition, with King George V also announcing at the famous Delhi Darbar on 12th December, that the capital of India would henceforth be Delhi and not Calcutta. Thus Dhaka once again relapsed into the position of a district town on 1st April 1912.

The Partition of India and the Birth of Bangladesh

With the end of the British rule in India and the creation of the sovereign states of India and Pakistan in 1947, Dhaka became the provincial capital of East Pakistan. In response to the need for accommodating newcomers, officers, and other heterogeneous population rushing to the city, Dhaka began to expand rapidly. The secretariat was established in the old Eden Girl's College building, the University quarters were requisitioned for high officials and ministers, while the Assembly Hall of the Jagannath Hall was used for the Legislative Assembly.

The anomaly of creating a country divided into two unequal wings was soon apparent. Protests against the declaration of Urdu as the sole language of Pakistan triggered violent protests. Police firing on the student demonstrators on 21st February 1952 led to the deaths of several students. This incident gave momentum to the language movement, leading gradually to the nationalistic movement and the birth of Bangladesh. In 1963 a Shahid Minar was built near the Medical College campus in commemoration of the martyrs of 1952. Destroyed in March 1971, the Shahid Minar was rebuilt in 1972.

Dhaka after the Liberation of Bangladesh

Immediately after independence, Dhaka accomplished rapid progress in recovering from war damages and economic and industrial set back. Foreign aid ushered in large amounts of money, and urban development activities were taken up in full swing.

As Dhaka became the capital of a new nation, it obviously experienced a rapid expansion of population, mostly due to large-scale migration from the countryside as well as repatriation from West Pakistan. According to an estimate, the population of Dhaka in 1990 was 6 million. It is predicted that Dhaka will have to accommodate almost 10 million people by the turn of the century. Such heavy influx of rural migrants, coupled with the scarcity of residential urban land, has led to the rampant growth of slums and squatter settlements in the city. A recent estimate indicates that there are about one million slums and squatter settlements in Dhaka city, constituting about one-third of the city's total population. The living conditions in slums are poor and sanitation facilities are almost non-existent. The city's piped water supply reaches only 67,000 houses and the sewerage system is connected to only 8,500 residences.

Due to rapid growth of population, the problem of housing also became acute in Dhaka. Prior to the independence of Bangladesh in 1971, most city dwellers were unwilling to live in flats or apartment houses. However, during the last decade, there has been a rapid change and more people are now thinking of living in apartment houses instead of expensive independent homes. There are at present about fifty developer companies in the city engaged in building highrise apartment complexes. Medium priced apartments are increasingly being purchased by the Bangladeshi wage-earners in the Middle-East. The development of highrise building complexes is concentrated in the central part of the city, specially Malibagh, Shantinagar, Eskaton, and Siddheswari areas.

Within the last decade or so, rapid urbanization of Dhaka has been characterized by the development of impressive shopping centres, elegant avenues, parks, gardens, amusement centres, and private hospitals. These splendid buildings, with their spectacular architecture, have markedly changed the skyline of the city.

FOLLOWING PAGE
Wall decoration on Sonargaon museum entrance.

Historic
Sonargaon

3

Historic Sonargaon

Sonargaon, a small sub-district lying seventeen miles northeast of Dhaka at the confluence of three major rivers - the Meghna, the Brahmaputra, and the Lakhya - was once the flourishing capital of Muslim Bengal in the middle ages. From the narratives of Chinese travellers who visited Sonargaon in the fifteenth century, we know that the city was well connected by sea routes with the middle and far eastern countries. It was well fortified with surrounding walls and was an important port city with broad roads and developed markets.

Sonargaon came into the limelight of history with the advent of Muslim rule in Bengal. In 667 Hijri, Emperor Balban of Delhi appointed Tughril Khan as the Governor of Bengal. Tughril Khan selected Sonargaon as his capital and built a fortress at 'Larikhol' or 'Narikilla' near Sonargaon from where he conducted campaigns against the kings of Tripura and Raja Danuj Rai of Sonargaon.

During the next three hundred years of Muslim reign in Delhi, Sonargaon was ruled by numerous governors, appointed by the emperor of Delhi under different dynasties. Many of these governors declared themselves as the independent kings and ran into conflict with the Sultanate of Delhi. When Ghiyasuddin Bahadur Shah of Sonargaon rebelled against Delhi Sultan Ghyiasuddin Tughlak in 1323, he was replaced by Nasiruddin Ibrahim and Sonargaon was taken over by Ghiyasuddin Tughlak.

In 738 Hijri, one of the commanders-in-chief, named Fakrah, occupied Sonargaon, assigned himself the title of Sultan Fakhruddin Mubarak Shah, and declared himself as the independent king of Sonargaon. During the ten years' rule by Fakhruddin Mubarak Shah, Sonargaon reached the peak of fame and glory as the capital city of medieval Bengal. Fakhruddin conquered Chittagong and estabestablished

extensive maritime communication with countries of southeastern Asia. We learn from the writings of Ibne Batuta, the famous traveller who visited Sonargaon at this time, that the capital city was flourishing with trade and commerce and had the highest level of administration. In 1349, Ikhtiaruddin Ghazi Shah succeeded Fakhruddin Mubarak Shah after his death. Shortly afterwards, one Haji Ilyas Shah captured Sonargaon and annexed the city with west Bengal. Subsequently, the capital was re-established at Sonargaon by Ghiyasuddin Azam Shah, a patron of scholastic activities and a great administrator, who established diplomatic relationship with distant countries like China, and had contacts with Persian poet Hafiz of Shiraj. Ghiyasuddin Azam Shah died in 1410 and was buried at Mograpara near Sonargaon. His tomb continues to attract lots of visitors.

The subsequent Iliyas Shahi Sultans who rose to power in Sonargaon were weak administrators. Ganesh, an ordinary civil servant, took advantage of this situation and captured power and declared himself as Raja Ganesh in 817 Hijri. He also shifted the capital of Bengal from Sonargaon to Lakhnauti. After a long period of political turmoil and upheaval, Ilyias Shahi Sultans and Hussain Shahi Sultans were re-established in Sonargaon. Subsequently, the capital was taken over by Sulaiman Karani of the Karani dynasty in 1565 AD.

In 1574, Emperor Akbar of Delhi sent his Commander-in-Chief, Munim Khan, to Bengal to combat Isa Khan Masnad-e-Ala, the leader of the Bara Bhuyias of Bengal. In 1594, Man Sing was made the Mughal Governor of Bengal, and came into confrontation with Musa Khan, the son of Isa Khan. Musa Khan made Sonargaon his capital and set up naval posts along the waterways of Meghna and Sitalakhya near Narayanganj.

In September 1606, Raja Man Singh was relieved of duty as the Governor of Bengal by the Mughal authority in Delhi, and two years ater (1608), Islam Khan was appointed the Subedar of Bengal Subah. In 1611, Islam Khan's chief admiral Mirza Nathan launched a severe attack on the strongholds of Musa Khan in Sonargaon and Narayanganj in which Musa Khan was defeated. Afterwards, Musa Khan fled away from the capital at Sonargaon, and his contingent surrendered to the Mughal army. Thus, Sonargaon came under the dynamic Mughal administration and remained so till 1763 when the British took over the Diwani of Bengal.

Scattered over the entire area of Sonargaon are numerous unidentified remains of mosques, tombs, *dargahs, khankahs,* and forts.

In today's Sonargaon proper, the village known as Painam contains many old and new buildings, which are believed to have been constructed by the Hindu *zamindars* and merchants of the area over the ruins of the defunct Muslim period. One can still see the traces of old fortifications and moats in many places along the streets of Painam. Many believe that this place, in its halcyon days, was the actual site of the lost capital of Sonargaon's legendary Sultans.

PRECEDING PAGE 22
Old mansion overlooking the pond in Sonargaon.

School children passing through the old street in
Painam village in Sonargaon.

TOP: Front view of the main entrance of the Sonargaon
Museum Complex.

Remnants of old building in Painam village still
providing shelter to many poor families.

Ruins of old building in the Sonargaon Museum
Compound.

An old piece of Mahogany furniture (cot) preserved in
the Sonargoan Museum.

TOP: Delicate motif made with cut pieces of china clay
on masonry wall.

PRECEDING PAGE
Side view of the entrance hall of Sonargaon Museum.

Old Town
and the River
Buriganga

4

Old Town and The River Buriganga

The old town, standing on the northeastern bank of the river Buriganga, is the exotic and most spectacular part of the sprawling city of Dhaka. It is characterized by a network of narrow lanes, by-lanes, and streets, crowded and jammed with heavy traffic most of the time.

In the early 17th century Dhaka was a small township along the river Buriganga. The area started developing from a small riverside port into a provincial capital following the arrival of the first Mughal Subedar Islam Khan Chisti in 1608/1610. Islam Khan transferred the capital of Bengal from Rajmahal to Dhaka and renamed the city Jahangir Nagar after Emperor Jahangir of Delhi. Islam Khan and his large army found scattered settlements along the river, southeast of Babu Bazar area, inhabited mostly by Hindu settlements, including Lakkshmi Bazar, Tanti Bazar, Sutrapur, Shankhari Bazar, Jalua Nagar, Bania Nagar, Goal Nagar, Kumartuli, Potuatuli etc. To the west of Babu Bazar, Islam Khan established a small fort (now Central Jail) and the surrounding areas, bearing Muslim names were developed into a 'new town'. The new settlement was separated from the old by a canal called the *Dolai Khal*, excavated at Islam Khan's initiatives. Chawk Bazar (old Badshahi Bazar) Islampur, Mogoltuli, Urdu Bazar, Bakhshi Bazar, and Diwan Bazar which developed during this time were predominantly inhabited by the Mughal elite and their local associates. The Islampur area, which lies parallel to the Buriganga river, was named after its founder Islam Khan. He also built a mosque at the north end of Islampur Road in Syed Awlad Hussain lane known as *Islam Khan-ki-Masjid*. The Islampur area is now the chief emporium of jewellery, textile, and watches.

During the Mughal rule, Dhaka experienced large-scale building activities. Mosques, monuments, and *katras* (public houses), built mostly along the river front, provided a magnificent view of the city's skyline from the river. The *Boro Katra* was built by Shah Shuja (1644) as an impressive caravanserai. It is a two hundred twenty-three feet long building, on an extensive area, on the bank of the river Buriganga. This magnificent building is an example of the classic Mughal architecture, consisting of a massive three-storeyed gateway in he centre, bounded by octagonal corner towers. Unfortunately, most of the building has decayed and only a small part of the central gateway is preserved in a dilapidated stage. Sometime in 1663, Shaista Khan built *Choto Katra*, close to the east end of *Boro Katra*. This was modelled on the architectural design of *Boro Katra*. There were a few other *katras* built during the Mughal period along the river, but now remembered only in name: Maya *Katra*, Nawab *Katra*, and Mukim *Katra*.

The Mughals also built numerous mosques all over the city. Among those that have survived are the Lalbagh Fort mosque (1678-1679) and Khan Mohammad Mridha's mosque (1704-1705) in Atish Khana. The Lalbagh Fort itself is another example of the great Mughal architecture. Prince Azam Shah started building this fort-cum-palace on the northern bank of Buriganga in 1678. A significant part of the fort has survived to date, and regular prayers are still held everyday in its 400-year-old mosque. Another monument, the magnificent Hussaini Dalan (House), built by Prince Azam Shah in classic Islamic architectural design, is still used by the Shia Muslim community as a centre for religious activities during the Islamic month of Muharram.

During the Mughal period, progressive development of the city attracted foreign merchants to set up their own establishments along the bank of the river Buriganga.

When European merchants started arriving in Dhaka, they also brought with them the religion of Christianity and established several churches in the old town area, some of which exist even today.

Portuguese Catholic traders were the first Christians who came to Dhaka and set up the Church of the Holy Assumption in Narinda (1628-1629). The entire Armanitola area was developed by the Armenian settlers who came during the 17th century and established *zamindaris* as well as businesses in this area. The well-known church in Armanitola is the contribution of the Armenian community.

The Armenian Church of the Holy Resurrection, located in Armenian Street was built in 1781 on the site of an old Armenian chapel and cemetery. The church has important resemblances with the mother church now in Armenia. Another church, named St. Thomas Anglican Church, was built in 1819 on Johnson Road, north of Bahadur Shah Park in a style similar to that of the parish churches in England. The Holy Cross Church in Laxmi Bazar was completed in 1898 as a cathedral having a two-storeyed tower pierced by Gothic windows as the characteristic feature. In the Narinda area stands the large Christian cemetery where most of the European members of the East India Company lie buried. The oldest grave in the cemetery is of Rev. Joseph Paget, Minister of Calcutta, who died in Dhaka in 1774 at the age of twenty-six. There is also the tomb of William Kerkman of the Dutch East India Company who died in 1774. This is the only surviving relic of the Dutch existence in Dhaka.

Nawabpur road is the busiest street in the old town, always jammed with vehicles of every description from dawn to dusk. The small stores are stocked with machinery parts and hardware; the items openly displayed for buyers to pick up as they like.

Exclusively residential areas are hard to find in the old town. The Wari area had been planned as a residential area for the middle class people by the then Dhaka Collector Frederick Wyer in the late 18th century. The entire land area, measuring twenty-seven acres, had been distributed among civil servants at a price of rupees six for each residential plot of one *bigha* (one-third of an acre) per year. Within three years of allotment, new houses sprang up. The Wari project provided the early example for the subsequent development of the urban housing projects of Dhanmondi, Uttara, and Gulshan model towns in the 1960s.

French merchants established trading posts for spices in the area called Farashgonj (Frenchgonj) where spices such as raw turmeric, ginger, garlic, and chilies are still sold wholesale.

Also along the river front in Farashgonj, lie the ruins of Ruplal House, originally built by the Armenians in the middle of the 19th century and later bought and renovated by Ruplal Das, an eminent merchant and scholar of Dhaka. This magnificent edifice is embellished with huge, ornamented Doric columns supporting a massive triangular overhead projection modelled on classical Greek style. In 1888, the British Viceroy Lord Dufferin and Lady Dufferin visited Dhaka, and the royal couple was given a grand reception in the central ball room of Ruplal House. The house was also well known as a centre of excellence for art and literature. Famous artists like Ustad Ghulam Ali, Uday Shanker, comedian Amritraj, and literateur Sarat Chandra Chattopadhyaya held regular sessions on art, music, and literature. The only rival of Ruplal House in fame and grandeur at that time was Ahsan Manzil. After the partition of India in 1947, Ruplal's family moved to Calcutta and the house was left unattended.

Ahsan Manzil palace on the bank of the Buriganga river was the symbol of aristocracy of the Nawabs of Dhaka during the middle of the 19th to the early 20th century. The original town house or *Rang Mahal* belonged to one Shaikh Enayetullah, the *zamindar* of Jalaldi in Faridpur district, who sold the house to French merchants in Dhaka. In 1835, the French resold it to Khawja Alimullah, the founder of the Nawab dynasty in Dhaka. In 1872, Nawab Khawja Abdul Gani, son of Nawab Alimullah, rebuilt the house and named it "Ahsan Manzil" after his son Nawab Khawja Ahsanullah. Ahsan Manzil has now been extensively renovated and converted into a museum.

In different locations in the old town, professionals and craftsmen with distinct social and cultural background have established their settlements. Shankhari Bazar is one such area. It consists of a very narrow lane, about three quarters of a mile long. Its two- to three- storeyed brick houses are predominantly inhabited by Hindu artisans specializing in the traditional conch shell industry.

Everyday at dusk, the neighbourhood is filled with the aroma of burning incense and the sound of the conch. Along the sidewalks of the street, old craftsmen work on shells, carefully polishing and cutting them into ornamental shapes with handmade saws. In the adjoining Tanti Bazar, no *tantis* (handloom weaver) live today. Instead, the small old houses are overcrowded with goldsmiths sitting on the floor with little lamps in front and tiny blowers in their mouths, crafting fine gold and silver jewellery of extraordinary delicacy and design. Buyers, mostly women, come along to buy, bargain, or exchange their ornaments with the goldsmith. The deal is conducted in a cordial family atmosphere, characteristic of Bengali society.

The English Seminary was established in June 1835, it later became the Dhaka Collegiate School in 1841 and was finally upgraded into Dhaka College in 1844. Almost fifty years later, Jagannath College was established by Kishori Lal Roy Chowdhury by upgrading Jagannath School. The famous Pogose School was established by an Armenian named N. P. Pogose in 1848. The Mitford Hospital, named after Robert Mitford, the first English Collector of Dhaka, was built along the northern bank of Buriganga in 1803.

At the northern end of Nawabpur Road stands Bahadur Shah Park where sepoys had been hanged by the British in 1857. After the coronation of Queen Victoria in 1858, the park came to be known as Victoria Park. There is another small monument inside the park erected by the British in memory of their friendship with Nawab Khawja Hafizullah who died in 1884. In the 1960s, a large central Mughal-style mausoleum was built as a memorial to the martyrs of the anti-British sepoy mutiny.

The river Buriganga forms the southern and western boundary of Dhaka. It has played an important role in the development of the city as a riverine trading post. Numerous country boats still ferry passengers across the river and many mechanised vessels provide riverine communication with the remote districts like Barisal, Khulna, Daudkandi, and Munshiganj.

Thousands of people are employed in riverine activities in and along the river Buriganga. The loading and unloading of large cargo vessels are primarily done by labourers who move up and down with head loads of merchandise. The Sadarghat terminal hums with activities of passengers, boatmen, *coolies,* and visitors along the four mile long river bank.

Boat building and repairing have become an important industry along the Zinjira side of the river bank. However, there is little fishing activities in the river, probably because of the water traffic congestion. Along the river banks, clusters of country boats operate as floating hotels and shelters for gypsies called *Badia* or *Bede* who move from place to place in search of work as hunters, snake-charmers and folk healers.

PRECEDING PAGES 32, 33
Scene from the Sadarghat River Terminal.

36

Ruins of Lalbagh Fort.

AN AERIAL VIEW OF LALBAGH FORT ON THE BANK OF THE RIVER BURIGANGA: The famous Lalbagh Fort was built by Prince Muhammad Azam Shah, the third son of Emperor Aurongzeb of Delhi. The prince started building this magnificent palace-cum-fortress in 1678 AD, but could not complete the construction. Nawab Shaista Khan, who succeeded Prince Azam, continued the work but again left it incomplete because of the premature death of his daughter, Iran Dukth alias Bibi Pari.

TOP: Tomb of Bibi Pari. Bibi Pari was a favourite daughter of the Mughal Subedar Nawab Shaista Khan and wife of Prince Muhammad Azam Shah. She died at an early age in 1684 and was buried here. Shaista Khan built this magnificent tomb with imported marble, black basalt, and sandstone in memory of his beloved daughter.

BOTTOM: Ruins of the Lalbagh Fort, southern gate.

TOP: Southern gate of Lalbagh Fort with the adjoining boundary wall. The architectural design of the gate is very similar to those of the Mughal fortresses found in Delhi and Agra in northern India.

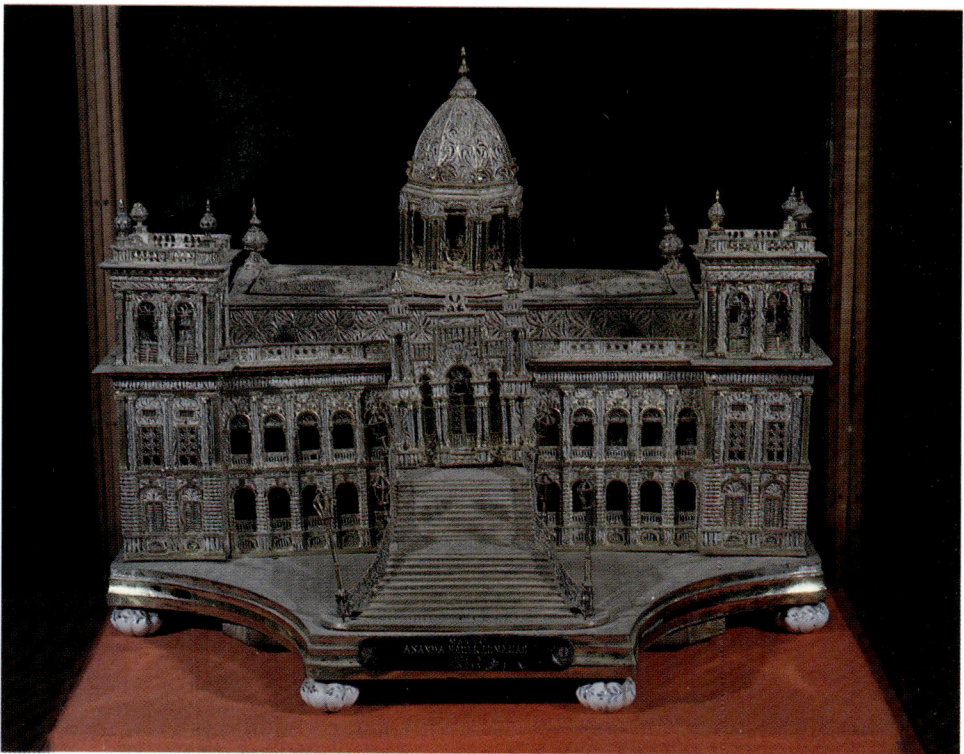

TOP: Ahsan Manzil, popularly known as the Nawab Bari, was said to have been built by one Shaikh Enayetullah, the Zamindar of Faridpur district in the early nineteenth century. Shaikh Enayetullah used the building as his Rang Mahal (Recreational Resort) and later sold it to the French East India Company. In 1835, Khwaja Alimullah, the founder of the Nawab family in Dhaka, purchased the house from the French officials and used it as his residence.

During the British rule, the building was used as a guest house for foreign dignitaries including Lord Curzon who visited Dhaka in 1904. The building was left unattended for many years. Recently, it has been extensively renovated and restored to original style and converted into a museum.

BOTTOM: Silver replica of Ahsan Manzil with delicate filigree work (Courtesy of National Museum, Dhaka).

TOP: Interior view of the Ahsan Manzil State Dining Hall.

BOTTOM: Finely decorated ornamental umbrella found in Ahsan Manzil.

FOLLOWING PAGE
TOP: *Hussaini Dalan* (Hossaini Building). Originally built during the 17th century, this building was rebuilt on its original site by Nawab Ahsanullah around 1897 and was the centre of all religious activities of the Shia Muslim community in Dhaka.

BOTTOM: Silver replica of *Hussaini Dalan* (Courtesy of Bangladesh National Museum, Dhaka).

FOLLOWING PAGE CENTREFOLD
An aerial view of the downtown Gulistan area.

PRECEDING PAGE
A craftsman making conch-shell ornament
in a factory in Shankhari Bazar lane.

TOP: Conch-shell being cut with a special saw.

TOP: Bullock carts carrying construction materials are common sights in the congested streets of the old town.

BOTTOM: In a store in Islampur, two men are leisurely browsing through the day's newspaper.

TOP: In a store on Islampur Road, a vendor weighing brass utensils before sale. Traditionally made brass and copper utensils for domestic use are very popular among the rural people.

BOTTOM: A tiny tea stall on Shankhari Bazar lane.

A goldsmith engraving fine details on jewellery in a
factory in Tanti Bazar lane.

TOP: A traditional restaurant specializing in biriani (rice cooked with butter oil or ghee and meat) near the Babu Bazar Police Station.

FOLLOWING PAGE CENTREFOLD
Babu Bazar rice market is the central supply depot of rice for the whole city. It is often called the rice-bowl of Dhaka. Different varieties of rice are procured from various rice growing areas of the country, particularly the north, and are distributed to the retailers through out the city from here.

TOP: Nawabpur Road in the old town is well known for machinery parts and hardware. Traffic congestion is a regular feature on this road.

FOLLOWING PAGE
Shankhari Bazar lane during the celebration of Durga Puja, the biggest religious festival of the Hindu community of Dhaka.

FRECEDING TWO PAGES
Rickshaw vans waiting to be hired by customers in front of an old building near Ahsan Manzil.

Bundles of sugarcane sticks being unloded near the Sadarghat terminal for distribution in the city.

TOP: Workmen unloading cargo at the Sawarighat.

FOLLOWING PAGE
Country boat being repaired on the bank of the river Buriganga.

61

TOP: A boat being repaired on the river bank during the early morning fog.
BOTTOM: A boy on his ferry boat at dusk on the Buriganga river.

PRECEDING TWO PAGES
TOP: A boatman with his ferry boat.
BOTTOM: Cement bags being carried on a country boat.

TOP: Spectators gathered on a launch during a rowing competition on the Buriganga.

BOTTOM: A scene from the rowing competition.

FOLLOWING APGE

TOP: Ferry boats awaiting along the Buriganga river near Wiseghat.

BOTTOM: A scene from the Sadarghat river terminal.

TOP: Cluster of country boats anchored along the river ghat in Zinjira.

BOTTOM: Passengers being carried on country boats across the Buriganga.

FOLLOWING PAGE
TOP: A bridge across the river Buriganga.

BOTTOM: A boatman with his country boat wating to ferry passengers across the Buriganga river.

The People

5

The People

The most distinctive, fascinating, and perplexing feature of Dhaka city is its human mass. No nook and corner of the metropolis is empty of people. People loiter, speed, squat, and puddle everywhere: on roads, lanes, and highways, along rail roads, under bridges, on station platforms and culverts, inside sewer pipes; in the shade or under the open sun.

Young boys and girls vending flowers on streetcorners, old men staggering under huge head-loads, drivers taking brisk naps on their wheels, executives carrying brief cases in their hands, service-men rushing for their buses, bureaucrats and industrialists relaxing inside their airconditioned cars, hawkers and petty vendors shouting at the top of their voices, unclad children defecating anywhere - all have one thing common: they belong to Dhaka.

Only the inhabitants of old Dhaka are considered the original native population. They are popularly known as *kutti* and speak a hybrid *kutti* language, a cross between local Bengali and Urdu dialects with a sing-song intonation all its own.

The greater part of the population consists of migrants, mainly rural migrants, who were driven out of their village homes by abject poverty, natural calamity, and unemployment. About seventy-five per cent of the heads of families at present were born outside the city. A small part of the population consists of Muslims from India - generally lumped as Biharis - who came in the wake of partition of India in 1947. While some non-Bengalis migrated to Pakistan, during the early 1970s, a significant number of Biharis still dwell in ghetto-like conditions in Mirpur and Mohammadpur areas of the city. Migration is still continuing, and at least forty per cent of the city's recent population growth is due to migration, mostly of the poor landless class.

Today, Dhaka is overwhelmed with people, significantly more than the city can support. In 1974, Dhaka had a population of 2.3 million. By 1981, it had grown to 3.7 million and, by 1991, to almost 7 million. It is projected that, by the turn of the century, Dhaka's population will be 11.2 million, making it the tenth largest city in the world.

But even these figures are a luxury when set against present truth. In today's Dhaka there are over 1,125 slums, and in each of these slums, each square mile houses more than 420,000 people. Less than a city, for these slum dwellers, Dhaka is a living hell.

In general, the people of Dhaka are fairly intelligent and are well aware of the developments in the modern world. Even the illiterate rickshawallas or the street urchins can identify the Hollywood, or the Bombay stars, the American President or the sport champions of the time.

PRECEDING TWO PAGES (CENTREFOLD)
Devotees of Biswa Ijtema in Tongi are washing and bathing in a nearby pond.

FOLLOWING PAGE
A young girl in Amin Bazar, Dhaka.

A happy family in a jolly mood.

A mother in Nandipara, near Dhaka, bathing her child
during a hot summer day.

Portrait of an old woman.

FOLLOWING PAGE
A Hindu *bostumi* (monk) in Dhakeswari temple.

TOP: Spectators gathered around the central Shahid Minar to watch an open stage drama on Shahid day, the twenty first February.

PRECEDING PAGE
A boy leisurely enjoying the warmth of the winter morning sun near the Mirpur bridge.

TOP: Women construction workers on the street of Dhaka.

BOTTOM: A destitute family taking shelter under the passengers' shade at a bus-stop.

81

A worker unloading cement bags at the Sadarghat
river terminal.

TOP: A rickshawalla leisurely grooming himself during recess in Motijheel.

BOTTOM: Balloon vendors in front of Dhaka Art College.

A hawker in the streets of Dhaka.

A member of a musical band playing his trumpet
during a performance at Dhaka Stadium.

A young man posing as a freedom fighter during a
dress-as-you-like competition organised by the
Parjatan Corporation.

Green coconuts being carried by a hawker for sale
near the Sadarghat river terminal.

An old man cooking his meal by the side of a road.

Procession of Dhaka University students celebrating
Bengali New Year's day.

FOLLOWING PAGE CENTREFOLD
New High Court Building

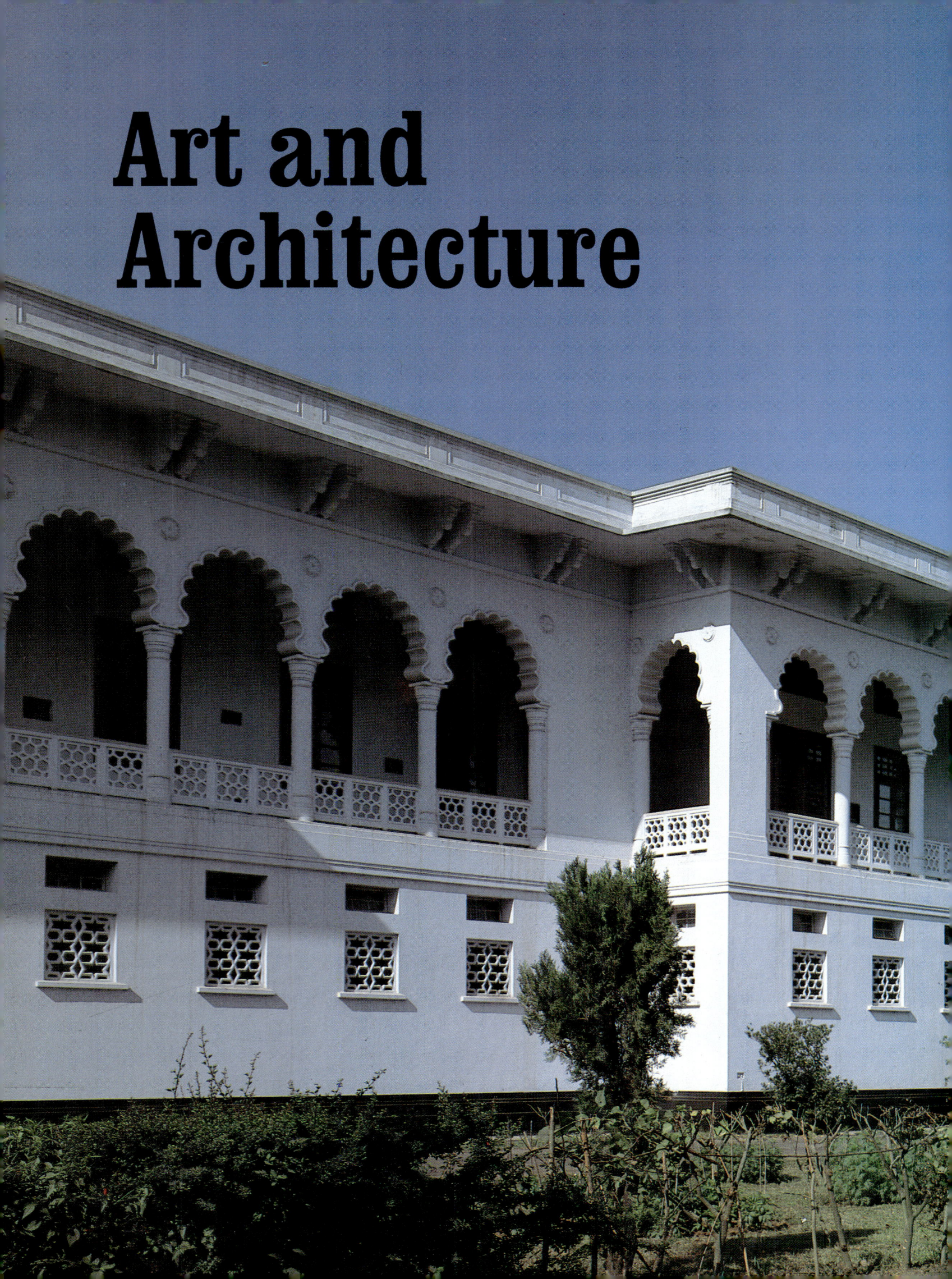

Art and Architecture

6

Art and Architecture

The history of art and architecture of Bengal may broadly be classified into four distinct periods. The first begins with the conquest of Bengal by the Muslims in 1205 and extends to 1575; the second covers the Mughal period between 1575 and 1757, the third phase covers the British period from 1757 to 1947, and the fourth covers the modern period following 1947.

Although the Muslim conquerors introduced certain common structural elements generally associated with Islamic architecture such as the arch, dome, *minar,* and *mihrab,* the style was considerably influenced by the local traditions as well as by the availability of indigenous building materials. The remoteness of Bengal from the Mughal capital in Delhi encouraged the development of independent art and architecture of Muslim Bengal largely in isolation, especially during the two centuries of rule by the independent Sultans of Bengal from 1338 to 1575. The two major confounding variables that played an important role in the development of architectural design in this region are climate and geography, which, more than anything else, conditioned the lifestyle, custom, and social behaviour of the people of this land.

The Pre-Mughal Period

In the pre-Mughal period, the development of architectural art was considerably influenced by the traditional Muslim style characterized by attractive interior decorations. The regional elements of style are reflected by a richness of surface decorations with terracotta floral art and an occasional use of intricate stone carving or glazed tile work. The traditional use of bricks, manufactured cheaply in abundance, remained the primary building material in the absence of stones. Heavy monsoon rain forced the builders to cover their edifices with multidome roofs rather than an open court, unlike those seen in upper India. Another striking indigenous architectural element evolved in this region is the distinct curvilinear roof form derived from the style of thatched huts, so common in rural Bangladesh. The pliant nature of the available indigenous building materials, including timber, bamboo, cane, and reed, greatly influenced the design of curvature of the roof and its cornice, which, when carried across its facade in a series of parallel curves, take the form of a bow. This typical element, derived from bamboo framework, was adopted to throw off heavy rains and to withstand the winds of the early monsoon. When these distinctive elements were incorporated into brick buildings, the result was often very elegant.

These features, often, termed as folk architecture, however, never rose to classical height. Nevertheless, the style often endowed the edifices with a freshness and spontaneity of its own, expressive of rural populace, keenly aware of the elements of nature affecting their lives. Traditionally, this distinctive curvilinear feature became a popular and attractive style emulated by many architects as far afield as Lahore, Agra, and even distant Rajputana between the 17th and 19th centuries.

The only surviving monument of the pre-Mughal period in Dhaka is Binat Bibi's mosque built in 1457 in Narinda. Other monuments of the Sultanate period around Dhaka are the single-dome Goaldi Mosque built by Hizabar Akbar Khan during the time of Sultan Husain Shah (1493-1519); the single-dome mosque of Fateh Shah at Mograpara, built during the reign of Sultan Jalaluddin Fateh Shah (1484); and the elegant six-dome mosque, popularly known as Baba Adam's mosque at Rampal (1483). This mosque has octagonal corner turrets, a gracefully curved cornice that is typical of the period, and both the facade and the three *mihrabs* are relieved with beautiful terracotta floral and hanging patterns.

The Mughal Period

During the Mughal period the indigenous features, such as the curvature of the roof and rich terracotta surface decorations of the Sultanate buildings, were replaced by straight horizontal cornice and plaster panels. During this period, the major elements introduced by the Mughal builders include dominant central domes and tall axial entrances, set in a central projecting bay for emphasis, while the entrances themselves were inset in taller half-domes.

Most of the surviving Mughal monuments are situated in and around Dhaka. Sir Charles D'Oyly, the British Collector of Dhaka and a gifted artist, painted in 1808, a series of sketches of Dhaka's old buildings, located mostly on the Buriganga waterfront. These sketches along with some descriptive texts were published in a book in London in 1830 entitled *The Antiquities of Dacca.* However, many of the monuments D'Oyly painted no longer survive. One of these defunct edifices was the mosque of Saif Khan, known to have been built during the reign of Jahangir on the site of a Hindu temple in the old area of the city.

The earliest Mughal monument in Dhaka is the *Idgah* (open field for Eid prayers) located in Dhanmondi. It was built by Mir Abul Qasim, the Diwan of Mughal Subedar Shah Shuja in 1640. It consists of a free-standing plastered screen wall on the west, accommodating a semioctagonal multicusped central *mihrab,* flanked on either side by multicusped panels within frames. It has now been renovated and enclosed on the other three sides with high boundary walls.

The next important monument in order of sequence is the majestic *Boro Katra*, situated on the northern bank of the river Buriganga near Chawk Bazar, also built by Mir Abul Qasim. It consists of a two-storeyed magnificent building with a 233-feet riverfront, approached through a monumental arched gateway in the middle. Originally, this noble monument with imposing octagonal corner towers enclosed a central courtyard, overlooked by four elegant blocks, each with 22 apartments which were probably a caravanserai, intended to provide resting places for travellers. A similar, but smaller, version of this, known as *Choto Katra*, was built by Nawab Shaista Khan in 1663, and is located about 200 yards east of *Boro Katra*.

The most imposing, but unfinished, monument of the Mughals is the Lalbagh Fort or Fort Aurangabad. It is situated on the southwest corner of the old city overlooking the river Buriganga. The construction of the fort was begun during the time of Emperor Aurangzeb in 1678 by Prince Muhammad Azam, the *Subedar* of Bengal. But his short tenure of office in Dhaka did not allow him to complete the building. His successor Shaista Khan resumed its construction, but he abandoned the work because of the premature death of his favourite daughter Bibi Pari, betrothed to Prince Azam.

All that survives today of this incomplete fort include a long rampart on the south and west with semi-octagonal bastions at intervals, two imposing gateways, on the north and south, a three-dome elegant mosque on the west, the tomb of Bibi Pari in the middle, a two-storeyed audience hall and a *hammam* (bath house) and a large tank on the eastern boundary.

The tomb of Bibi Pari is a unique monument where precious foreign stones were used for the first time in Bengal. These include black basalt from Rajmahal and white marble and glazed tiles from Rajputana, which were used for embellishing its nine chambers. Curiously, the roofs of all chambers are spanned by overlapping courses of massive black basalt slabs, while the central tomb-chamber, entirely encased in marble, is covered by a false copper dome.

The Sat Gombuj Mosque in Jafarabad area, west of Mohammadpur, believed to have been erected by Shaista Khan, illustrates a fine example of the Mughal architectural design in Bangladesh in the 17th century. The prayer hall of this oblong building, situated picturesquely on the edge of a low lying flood plain, is surmounted by three bulbous domes and has four hollow octagonal corner towers, each crowned with a large cupola. From this appearance it derives its name Sat or seven-dome mosque, but actually it is a three-dome mosque.

Another typical example of architecture during Shaista Khan's reign is the three-dome mosque behind the old High Court building, built in 1679 by Haji Khwaja Shahbaz, a wealthy merchant of Dhaka. Its prayer chamber is divided into three square bays with two multi-cusped lateral arches and three *mihrabs* on the western wall, embellished with spearhead cusping and floret spandrels. The corner towers are gracefully capped by ribbed cupolae.

The mosque of Khan Muhammad Mridha, located close to the northwest corner of the Lalbagh Fort in an area still known as Atishkhana, is an interesting monument which was built in 1706. It is a two-storeyed building with a series of vaulted chambers on the ground floor, while the three-dome oblong mosque is located on the upper floor. Its corner minarets rise higher than the parapet and terminate in ribbed cupolae.

The only parallel to the Mridha's two-storeyed mosque is the five-dome Kartalab Khan's mosque at Begum Bazar, near the Central Jail. This mosque was built by Nawab Murshid Quli Khan, alias Kartalab Khan, between 1700 and 1704. It has a graceful *dochala* (two-sided roof) hut-shaped room along its northern face which, with its curvilinear eaves, gives a very distinctive look. Facing the mosque on the east, across a narrow street, is what once used to be known as a *Baoli* or stepped-well in Bangladesh, now completely choked with debris. A flight of steps leads down to the water level at the bottom of the *Baoli.*

The present Hussaini Dalan (House), situated behind the Dhaka Medical College campus, was originally built during the later part of the Mughal rule in Dhaka as the *Imambara,* where Shia religious ceremonies are held during the Muslim month of Muharram of the Islamic calendar. The two large halls, known as Shirni Hall and Khutba Hall, are placed back- to-back to form the nucleus of the edifice. After a devastating earthquake in 1897, it was rebuilt by Nawab Ahsanullah Bahadur in 1898. The present flat roof and verandah, carried on a series of Doric columns, were added at the time of its reconstruction.

The Chawk Jami Mosque, according to an inscription found on the building, was originally built by Nawab Shaista Khan in 1676. It has now been so extensively renovated and extended that it is difficult to trace its original features. Originally, it was a three-dome rectangular building which stood on a high podium with a series of chambers underneath.

The dainty little Star Mosque at Armanitola has an inlaid star pattern made of broken pieces of china. Originally, it was a three-dome mosque, built by Mirza Ghulam Pir in the early 18th century, but about a century back, a local businessman, named Ali Jan Bepari, added a verandah on the east and redecorated the mosque with Japanese and English china clay tiles. But recently, the mosque has been extensively renovated by demolishing a part of the edifice, giving it the appearance of a five-dome mosque with a large one alternated by smaller domes.

Among a series of river fortresses built in the 17th century to protect the water routes to Dhaka, the Idrakpur Fort in Munshiganj, about 15 miles southeast of Dhaka, is a typical example. It is an oblong fortress with a circular bastion at each corner, filled solidly with earth to rampart level, above which runs the battlemented parapet, liberally pierced with loop holes for musketry. A striking feature of this fort, common to others of the group, is an enormous round bastion facing the river, meant for mounting a high-calibre cannon. Two others of the series on either bank of the Sitalakhya river are to be found at Hajiganj; one of which, by planning is a pentagon, and the other at Sonakanda in Narayanganj is rectangular in ground structure.

Ibrahim Khan II (1689-1697), the son of Ali Mardan Khan, built a palace-cum-fort at Zinjira opposite *Boro Katra*, across the Buriganga river. Ghaseti Begum and Amina Begum, the aunt and mother of Nawab Sirajuddaula, were kept confined here for a while before being drowned in the river by the order of Miron, the assassin of Siraj. The fort is now in utter ruins, heavily encroached by slum dwellers of the locality. The only surviving part of it is a dilapidated gateway and an elaborate *hammam* (bath house).

The renovated Dhakeswari temple near Lalbagh does not appear to be older in architectural style than what prevailed in the 17th century. The first group of the Dhakeswari temple complex consists of four spired temples with six deeply curved receding mouldings in plaster, each being a shrine by itself. The second group on the east has three pyramidal *sikhara,* each crowned with pinnacles. The *sikharas* consist of four receding tiers, the first of which is domeshaped with a curvilinear roof, and the remaining three are of the north Indian Pida type, all capped by a lotus finial.

Among different categories of arts which flourished under the Muslim rule in this country, wood carving and brass industry attained a high standard of perfection. However, painting in this extremely humid region was never very popular. A few specimens of the paintings of Muharram processions and similar other subjects, preserved in the National Museum, are of a later date and display a decadent style.

The art of calligraphy or penmanship in various forms, including the Arabic and the Persian scripts, was practiced in Bengal with skill and ingenuity. Of these, at least five varieties, the Tughra style flourished here. The excellence and skill with which these items were made have no parallel in the entire world of Islam. The style is purely decorative with the scribe arranging the words and letters of the text, not in order of sequence, but randomly. In its bow-and-arrow variety, also known as boat and war, marching of soldiers, congregation of the faithful, etc., the letters with curvative designs are written across the body of the shafts in the shape of a bow or boat. The specimens of Kufic or the earliest angular calligraphy, including those varieties which flourished around Delhi, Agra, and other important places in upper India, such as Suls, Naskh, Tughra, and Nastaliq, are frequently encountered. A few excellent specimens of the period found in Dhaka are the Binat Bibi's mosque inscription (1457) at Narinda, the *Boro Katra* inscription, and the inscription found at the Bibi Pori's tomb in Lalbagh Fort.

Architecture during the British Period

The style of architecture during the British colonial period (1757-1947) passed through a succession of the changing phases. The late European renaissance idea came to be adopted here in the 17th and 18th century, particularly in the building of churches in Dhaka - such as the Church of St. Nicholas Tolentino built in 1663, the Holy Rosary Church at Tejgaon (1677), Armenian Church of the Holy Resurrection (1781), and the Anglican Church on Johnson Road (1819). All of these were, however, extensively renovated subsequently. Later, the style was applied to secular buildings, some of which may still be seen in the Wiseghat locality of old Dhaka.

In the late 18th and early 19th centuries, another style, in which buildings were given semi-octagonal or rounded corners with tall Doric columns, gained popularity. The classical Greco-Roman architecture, adopted in medieval Europe and classified under Tuscan, Doric, Ionic, Corinthian, and composite titles, became very popular in Bangladesh. The examples may be studied on a series of feudal palaces in the outlying areas and some state buildings of Dhaka. Some of these, including the *zamindar* palaces at Baliati, Puthia, and Dubalhati, bear a striking resemblance to the famous Senate House in Cambridge, England (1722-1730), but considerably enriched with local elements. The new architectural features, introduced during the 19th century, were the semi-circular arch, triangular pediment carried over semi-corinthian, Doric or Ionic columns, and other foliated motifs in plaster. A typical example of it is the imposing Ahsan Manzil of the Nawabs of Dhaka

Another magnificent two-storeyed building, popularly known as the Rose Garden Lodge in the Narinda locality, was built in the 19th century by a Hindu *zamindar* named Hrisikesh Das. This building is another fine example of the renaissance style in Dhaka. The building has an imposing western facade with its prominently projecting central bay which is retrieved with four tall Corinthian columns, shooting up to the second floor. The central part of the edifice carries a hemispherical overhead dome which rests on octagonal neck, consisting of a series of short Corinthian columns, alternated by semi-circular arches. The cornice over the two ends are relieved with two prominent triangular pediments, containing an insignia of a crown and two flags on either side of a round plaque. Other examples of this style of architecture are the old High Court building, originally designed to be a Government House and the elegant little Greek memorial located within the Dhaka University campus.

In the late 19th and early 20th century, a new hybrid of the Mughal and the European building style emerged in the wake of the first partition of Bengal (1905), mainly under the influence of Lord Curzon, a great admirer of Mughal art and architecture. The notable examples of this syncretic trend may be seen in the Northbrook Hall, Curzon Hall, Dhaka Medical College Hospital, and Salimullah Muslim Hall. Among these, the most elegant two-storeyed Curzon Hall, founded by Lord Curzon in February 1904 as a Town Hall, represents a fascinating facade with its central projecting bay and wide portals with horse-shoe arches. Its elevation is variegated by a series of panels, bracketed eaves, and kiosks, while the corners are relieved with *minars* and corridors provided with fretted screens.

The Modern Period

Partition of the British India into India and Pakistan in 1947 immediately heralded an era of building activities to fulfil the need of the expanding capital of East Pakistan in Dhaka. The new buildings were mostly of the utilitarian types common to all modern cities, bereft of the splendour of the old monuments, the idea and purpose being the creation of maximum space with minimum cost and time. Characteristics of these modern buildings are the liberal use of reinforced concrete for highrise structures with straight horizontal and vertical lines dominating the skyline. These buildings are mostly concentrated in the Motijheel Commercial Area and include the Sena Kalyan Bhaban (Army Welfare House), Bangladesh Bank building complex, Shilpa Bank building, Jiban Bima Bhaban, Janata Bank Tower, Adamjee Court, the Secretariat (Eden Building), etc.

However, there are some silver linings in the new trends of the stereotyped architecture. The Bait-ul-Mukarram Mosque, the largest of the modern mosques in the country, is one such bold concept translated into masonary form. The main four-storeyed prayer hall has been designed in the form of a large cube, modelled on the shape of the Holy Ka'aba in Mecca, while the cloisters and the main entrance hall bear elegant arches, domes, and fretworks as elements of traditional Islamic architecture. The other successful edifices of the out-of-the-ordinary are the Bangabhaban (Government House), the grand new High Court building, the Kamlapur Railway Station, and the National Memorial at Savar.

The Bangabhaban and the imposing High Court building are each dominated by a graceful bulbous central dome and a facade, tastefully embellished with multicusped arches. Although both the buildings carry the Mughal architectural style and tradition in their outward appearence, they are internally provided with all modern amenities.

The Kamlapur Railway Station building is, however, a departure from anything built so far in this country. A feeling of space and openness probably was the uppermost consideration in the mind of the architect when designing this splendid building complex that appears flying up in the sky from a distance. Its roof rests on a forest of slender re-enforced concrete columns, mostly open on all sides while a series of eye-catching cusps, emulating lotus petals at the roof, break the skyline.

The National Memorial at Savar commemorates the martyrs who laid down their lives in 1971 to achieve the independence of Bangladesh. The edifice consists of a series of graded huge louvers of concrete, tapering a hundred and fifty feet high to a needle sharp point, surrounded by a beautifully laidout terraced garden and a reflecting pool of water.

Shapla Chattar island at night in Motijheel Commercial Area.

96

A woman wearing a *Jamdani* sari. Dhaka is well known for its characteristic *Jamdani* sari. These colourful saris with their distinctive design and texture are manufactured by skilled weavers using fine cotton or silk yarn. Spinning, weaving, and dyeing are all done by members of a family, professionally skilled in the trade.

PRECEDING PAGE: *Jamdani* weavers at work in the village of Dakhkin Rupasi, Kanchpur, Dhaka.

TOP: Two girls spinning cotton yarn for *Jamdani* sari in the village of Dakhkin Rupasi in Kanchpur near Dhaka.

A bride wearing a *katan* sari, the most popular
wedding costume in Bangladesh.

A woman hand-spinning fine silk yarn for weaving *katan* sari in Mirpur. Traditional *katan* saris are very popular as wedding outfits among Bangladeshi women. In Mirpur, *katan* saris are woven in most houses.

TOP: Fine woodwork on the head-board panel of an old cot found in the Dhaka region (Courtesy: National Museum, Dhaka).

FOLLOWING PAGE
TOP: Art objects created with dry coconut shell (left). Dolls made with old fabrics depicting rural women of Bangladesh (right).

BOTTOM: Examples of fine vessels made with bamboo trunks.

Finely carved, hand-made clay pots. These beautiful
pots come in various shapes, sizes, and colour. They
are locally manufactured by skilled craftsmen in Rayer
Bazar.

TOP: Finely decorated dolls made with old fabric.

BOTTOM: Young craftsman engraving fine details of old Victorian design on teak wood furniture in a factory in Badda.

TOP: National Memorial at Savar: This splendid monument is situated on the Dhaka-Aricha highway, 34 km from the city. It was built in 1982 as a memorial for the martyrs of the liberation war of 1971. The structure has a broad base with seven concrete louvers which shoot up to a height of 150 feet, ending into a needle-sharp point. The monument is surrounded by a beautiful garden and a huge reflecting pool of water in front.

BOTTOM: Lateral view from the west side of the National Memorial.

Masonry sculpture erected in memory of the martyrs
of the liberation war in front of the Dhaka University
Art's Building.

Curzon Hall: The foundation stone of this magnificent building was laid by Lord Curzon, the British Viceroy, on 14 February 1904, during his visit to Dhaka. Architecturally, it is an example of classical Anglo-Indian style, blended with a touch of Islamic tradition. The building was initially used as a Town Hall and later as the library of Dhaka College. Now it houses the science departments of Dhaka University.

Chemistry Department Building, Dhaka University:
This splendid building is situated in the Dhaka
University science campus next to Curzon Hall, to
which it bears striking similarities of structure and
decoration.

TOP: Chameri House (originally Chummery House). This English cottage-type building was constructed during the early eighteenth century as the residence for the British bachelor officials in Dhaka. The building now houses the CIRDAP office near the Dhaka University science campus.

TOP: Old Greek memorial located inside the Dhaka University campus.

BOTTOM: Side view of the memorial showing scripts in Greek.

FOLLOWING PAGE
TOP: *Old High Court building.* This renaissance-style building was constructed during the early part of the twentieth century as the official residence of the Governor of the newly created province of Bengal and Assam in 1905. In 1947, the building was used to accommodate the High Court of the newly formed Pakistan. Now it is used as the office of the Defence Ministry.

BOTTOM: *New High Court building.* Built during the later part of the twentieth century, modelled on the style of the old High Court building nearby.

Ruplal House, a nineteenth-century mansion, was built
in classic Greek style on the bank of the river
Buriganga in Farashgonj.

TOP: Bangladesh Bank and the Sena Kalyan Bhaban: These two high-rise buildings, built during 1960s and 1980s respectively, in the Motijheel Commercial Area, are examples of modern styles of contemporary architecture.

PRECEDING PAGE
TOP: An old *zamindar* house on Aga Sadek Road in the old town.

BOTTOM: Detailed view of the surface decorations on the house.

FOLLOWING TWO PAGES (CENTREFOLD)
An aerial view of the Fakirapool extension area.

TOP: Bangladesh Bank building in the Motijheel
Commercial Area illuminated on Victory Day.

FOLLOWING PAGE
Shapla Chattar (Lotus Circle), an important and busy
intersection in the Motijheel Commercial Area
(business district).

TOP: *Bangabhaban* (President's House) in Motijheel.

BOTTOM: City Corporation Building in Gulistan.

TOP: Kamlapur Railway Station. This splendid building enclosed under overhead cusps was built during early 1960s. It is the main railway station in the city.

FOLLOWING PAGE 122
This magnificent building standing along the Dhanmondi lake, is surfaced externally with red tile and bricks, having tall conical towers, simulating Chinese architecture.

FOLLOWING PAGE 123
TOP: Baitul Mukarram Mosque. This is the largest mosque in the country built in lean Mecca style during the early 1960s.

BOTTOM: Front view of the Baitul Mukarram mosque.

124

TOP: Khawja Amber Tomb: Situated near the old High Court building, this three-dome tomb-cum-mosque was built during the late seventeenth century. Adjacent to the tomb, there is a small structure in the form of a hut, typically found in rural Bangladesh.

PRECEDING PAGE
TOP: Qassabtuly Jam-e-Masjid in old town.

BOTTOM: Interior decoration of Qassabtuly mosque.

TOP: Mosque of Khan Mohammad Mridha (1704): This is one of the well-preserved Mughal mosques, situated in Atishkhana near the Lalbagh Fort. The mosque was built by Khan Mohammad Mridha in the traditional Mughal style, characterised by a three-dome structure.

FOLLOWING PAGE
TOP: Sat Gombuj Mosque (late seventeenth century). This mosque, situated in Mohammadpur was built by the Mughal Subedar Nawab Shaista Khan in 1680. Though it is called Sat Gombuj or seven-dome, it has in fact only three domes.

BOTTOM: An old, pre-Mughal, single-dome mosque in Azimpur Colony.

TOP: Dhakeswari temple complex in the old town.

BOTTOM: Hindu temple near the Dhaka University campus.

FOLLOWING PAGE
Armenian Church in Armanitola. This church was built in 1781 by the Armenian community who lived in Dhaka and became influential businessmen of the city.

TOP: Attractive and colourful cinema banners are common sights in front of the movie houses in Dhaka.

PRECEDING PAGE: Stone sculpture situated inside Armenian church compound.

Life in the
Streets

7

Life in the Streets

Amid the dreary flood of rickshaws, trucks, buses, and pedestrians, an old man tries to steer through the traffic, a young girl runs back and forth between cars selling flowers, a vendor sells fish, a woman boils rice, an old man peacefully takes a nap, a politician addresses a public gathering, a hawker crushes sugar cane juice, a group of men or women observe a hunger strike for their demands, a group of actors stages a political drama, a family sets up house at a bus stand, defecating, urinating, and giving birth.

The streets of Dhaka are not only used for the movement of traffic, but also to provide shelter for millions of uprooted, rural refugees, to render business opportunities for petty traders, and finally to provide unrestricted space for garbage disposal.

It is hard to name a commodity or service that is not available on the streets of Dhaka. You can easily buy a Christian Dior (fake ?) product or a pair of live buffaloes or have your fortune told by trained parrots or have a clean shave or haircut sitting right in the middle of the street at any time of the day.

The streets of Dhaka, particularly the old city, are probably the safest in the world, because of being most populous and congested. Although organized services are hardly available, yet emergency help is instantly provided in most critical times. If your car breaks down in the middle of the traffic any time during the day or night, don't worry. Stand-by personal services are always there. Poor, half-clad street urchins, locally called *tokai*, are standing by to help you tow your car to the nearest garage and to send the information to your home.

During the *hartals* when motorized traffic comes to a standstill, nothing except rickshaws play. People walk to their work and the whole city slows down. Once the *hartal* is over, the streets of Dhaka pulsate with traffic once more.

There are traffic regulations in Dhaka as elsewhere in the modern world, but the traffic here moves in its own way, occasionally winking at the law or the nonchalant policeman on the street. Signals are ignored, left turns blocked, fast-moving vehicles overtaken by rickshaws, and intersections clogged for hours, horns and whistles creating a deafening situation.

The street scene changes with the changing seasons. During the long, wet monsoon months, there are few activities along the sidewalks. Long rows of rickshaws fight against the rain and the wind, shattering the silence with the sounds of their jangling bells. But one scene hardly ever changes. No matter whether it is hot summer, wet monsoon or cold winter. A frail little girl will always greet you at every street corner with a bundle of fresh and fragrant, white *rajanigandhas* in her hand, softly asking *Saab ekta ful kinben?* (Sir, would you please buy a piece of flower?).

PRECEDING PAGE (CENTREFOLD)
A scene from the street in front of the New Market.

A double-decker bus over-loaded with passengers,
some hanging on for dear life.

Hundreds of rickshaws rushing ahead as soon as the light changes at the intersection of Airport Road and Bangla Motor.

FOLLOWING PAGE
TOP: Rickshaws, buses, and Thelagari still plying on Kakrail Road during a heavy downpour.

BOTTOM: A poor rickshawalla sleeping on his craft in a winter morning on the Mirpur Road.

TOP: An old man wading through waters in front of the Azimpur Gate of New Market.

BOTTOM: A young *tokai* (street urchin) with his sack on his way to collect recyclable house refuse.

TOP: Two cheerful *tokais* selling flowers in Sher-e-Bangla Nagar.

BOTTOM: Two *tokais* taking brisk nap in the shade along Bangabandhu Avenue.

PRECEDING PAGE
TOP: A man hawking old knit wool on the sidewalk near Ramna Bhaban in the Gulistan area.

BOTTOM: Old, hand-made box cameras are still used for cheap portraits, specially in the old town.

TOP: An old man selling green coconuts in front of Ahsan Manzil in old town.

Young women making garlands along Katabon Road.
Freshly picked tropical flowers are sold at most street
corners in the city throughout the year. Garlands of
yellow marigolds are specially prepared by young
women for sale during the winter.

TOP: Near Mohakhali Rail Gate, crowds of people rushing for the *Akheri Munajat* (concluding prayer) at Tongi *Biswa Ijtema*.

BOTTOM: Procession of demonstrators on Bangabandhu Avenue during a *hartal* (strike).

143

A man selling freshly extracted sugar cane juice in
front of the University Mosque near the Public Library.

Shadhana Ausadhalaya, a pharmacy outlet in
Sutrapur. It is the oldest Ayurvedic pharmaceutical
industry in the country.

TOP: Attractive pots made with burnt clay of various sizes and shapes are being sold on Mirpur Road.

BOTTOM: A traffic island on the intersection of Naya Bazar and Tanti Bazar in the old town.

A young boy selling colourful balloons in front of
Shishu Park.

Rear view of a beautifully decorated rickshaw.

A scene from the crowded Nawabpur Road and
Bangabandhu Avenue.

TOP: A row of baby taxis near Naya Bazar in the old town.

BOTTOM AND THE FOLLOWING PAGE: People carrying loads in *thelagari* (push carts) in Naya Bazar.

The Bazars

8

The Bazars

For setting up a Bazar, all one needs, is a place to sit and spread out a sheet with some commodities. The place will in no time attract several colleagues of the trade as well as customers eager for a bargain. *Kacha Bazars* (grocery markets) provide special attractions: they sell groceries, meat, fish, and fresh vegetables. Ask for a kilo of beef or a whole portion of a goat shoulder or leg; it will be chopped there right from the carcass. Grocery prices in Dhaka are probably the cheapest in the world: only one-and-a-half US dollars for a kilo of good beef, thirty cents for a kilo of rice and five cents for a kilo of potatoes.

The Bazars are always abundantly stocked with seasonal produce: spectacular heaps of mouth-watering melons in early summer; red lichees and luscious mangoes during the monsoon; and fresh green vegetables in winter.

During winter, the sidewalks of the main streets are filled with imported old clothes. They are important and attractive shopping centres for the city's poor and middle classes. Numerous long rows of colourful garments along the sidewalks in the street stretch in all directions in the Gulistan area. These shops are euphemistically called the "Nixon Market" because the old garments were first imported from the United States when Richard Nixon was the president of America.

Special winter markets called *Meena Bazars* are also organized by different social groups and clubs in various parts of the city. These Bazars provide opportunities for social gathering of the upper middle-class families as well as sale and introduction of home-made items including embroidered clothes, garments, jewellery, pottery etc. During the month of Ramadan, the holy month of fasting for the Muslims, special *iftar* items for breaking the fast, are sold along the sidewalks in the late afternoon. Varieties of hot, spicy, and attractive delicacies including *halim, piazu, beguni, samocha, jilapi* and other take-away foods are prepared and sold on the spot.

One cannot probably miss or actually avoid the cheerful *mintis,* who carry bamboo-baskets, trailing the shoppers and providing porter services at every Bazar. They are the substitutes for the shopping carts of the western supermarkets.

PRECEDING PAGE
A man weighing red chilies in Karwan Bazar market.

TOP: Used winter clothings are being sold on the sidewalks along the streets in Gulistan area.

BOTTOM: A petty vendor selling *garam masala* (hot spices) on the streets of Motijheel Commercial Area.

PRECEDING PAGE
TOP: Winter morning market in Malibagh. Fresh green vegetables are special attractions during the winter season.

BOTTOM: Heaps of colourful ground spices are on sale along the streets in Motijheel Commercial Area.

TOP: A tiny grocery shop in Mohammadpur Bazar.

BOTTOM: A pavement shop in New Market displaying varieties of caps.

FOLLOWING PAGE

TOP: Rows of shops displaying eggs in the open market in Malibagh.

BOTTOM: *Muri* (pop-rice) shops in the wholesale market in Karwan Bazar.

156

TOP: Grocery shops in Gulshan Municipal Market.

BOTTOM: A tiny banana shop in Mouchak market.

FOLLOWING PAGE

TOP: Cattle market in Gabtoli, near Mirpur.

BOTTOM: Colourful and attractive *gamchha* (short scarf) being sold near the Sadarghat River Terminal.

TOP: Giant grape fruits are being sold on the streets of Gulistan.

CENTREFOLD (Left)
A fruit shop along the street near the New Market. During the monsoon harvesting season, varieties of mangos arrive in the market and create special attraction for the consumers.

TOP: Fish market in Mohammadpur Bazar. A man is displaying *hilsha* fish, the most popular of all tropical fresh water fishes in the country.

FOLLOWING PAGE
TOP: A man is weighing fruits with his traditional scale in Mohammadpur Bazar.

BOTTOM: Fish is being processed right on the spot by a typical fish seller in the New Market.

A vendor in New Market displaying cut water melons
to attract customers.

A man hawking *chanachur* in front of the Sishu Park
(Children's Park). *Chanachur* is a very popular   snack
in Bangladesh. It is prepared by freshly mixing many
varieties of cereals, spices, and nuts and is flavoured
with fresh lemon.

The Festivals

9

The Festivals

Bengalis are well known for their love of festivals. As the popular saying puts it: "Bengal has thirteen festivals in twelve months". The Bengali calendar is replete with dates marked for one or the other cultural occasion.

Bangladesh observes national, seasonal, and religious festivals of both Muslims and Hindus. Religious functions of the minority Christians and Buddhists are also important events.

Eid-ul-Fitr is the most important annual celebration of the Muslims. It is observed on the conclusion of the holy month of Ramadan, marking the end of the month-long fasting and abstinence. On Eid day, colourful illuminations decorate the city squares and the buildings are decorated with attractive signs, banners, and festoons. Community prayers are held in open spaces and mosques, sweet dishes are prepared in most homes for sharing among the relatives and distribution to the poor.

Next to Eid-ul-Fitr, Eid-ul-Azha, or the festival of sacrifice, is the most important occasion for Muslims. It is observed seventy days after Eid-ul-Fitr. On this occasion, cows, goats, and sheep are sacrificed in a re-enactment of the sacrifice of prophet Ibrahim (R), and the meat distributed among relatives, friends, and the poor. Nearly fifty thousand animals are sacrificed in the city on this day.

Another special religious gathering which has been taking place in Dhaka as a regular annual event for many years is the *Biswa Ijtema.* This annual religious event attracts nearly three hundred thousand Muslims from all over the world, to the banks of the Turag in Tongi, near Dhaka. Despite the obvious difficulties of camp life, the congregation discusses, analyzes, interprets, and disseminates the teachings of Islam.

Muharram is another religious occasion of the Muslim community, commemorating the supreme sacrifice for truth and justice by Hazrat Imam Hussain (R) and Hazrat Imam Hassan (R), the two grandsons of the prophet Muhammad (SM) in the desert of Karbala. Mourning processions are brought out on the streets of Dhaka by the Shia Muslim community. Spectacular demonstrations take place, while the *tazia,* a big horse-drawn chariot, is pulled along the street, with the mourners flagellating themselves. The Sunni Muslims also bring out processions in remembrance of events which took place in the month of Muharram long before the martyrdom at Karbala.

Every year, the Hindu community of Dhaka celebrate the Durga Puja with utmost religious fervour. The Dhakeswari temple in the old city attracts thousands of Hindus who go there with their young and old to pay homage to the goddess Durga, as well as other goddesses. Besides, Durga, there are other goddesses, including Kali and Swaraswati.

The Bengali calendar begins in mid-April with the month of *Baisakh.* In 1993, the Bengali calendar completed the 14th century and entered into the 15th. This grand occasion was celebrated with great enthusiasm and cultural fervour. *Pahela Baisakh* or the first day of the *Baisakh* month begins with a huge gathering of people of all ages and sexes at the Ramna garden under the shade of the great banyan tree in the early morning mist every year. Women wear traditional yellow saris with red borders on the day and adorn their hair with garlands of fragrant white jasmine and men dress in silk *punjabis.* Members of sociocultural organizations perform open air concerts, the audience listening to the concert and eating traditional food, particularly *panta bhat* (cooked rice that has been soaked in water overnight).

Baisakhi mela, held during the month of *Baisakh*, is also the summer festival that is celebrated with great enthusiasm to welcome the season. *Baisakh* is also the season of storm and rain following a long spell of dry and cool winter. Similarly, the *Poush mela* or the winter festival is held during the Bengali month of *Poush.* It is characterized by varieties of open air activities, including live art performances and displays of traditional handicrafts. Throughout the winter (December to February), which is relatively mild in Dhaka, the city takes on a festive look. Because of the fair and pleasant weather many outdoor activities are organized throughout the winter season. Events like sports, flower shows, art performances, *jatras* (folk drama), *meena bazars,* magic shows, picnics, and other recreational activities dominate the cultural environment of the season.

Bengal has six seasons, of which *Basanta* or spring is the last. Coming at the end of winter, the Bengali month of *Falgun* heralds spring. *Basanta Utsab* or the spring festival celebrates the romantic season. Groups of young girls, wrapped in red-bordered yellow saris with fragrant flowers tucked in their hair, perform open air concersts-the main attraction of the *Basanta Utsab.*

Among the national holidays, the most important perhaps is the twenty-first February, the day when homage is paid to the martyrs of the language movement of 1952. The occasion begins at midnight with laying of wreaths at the central Shahid Minar near the Medical College campus. The day-long programme organized by various sociocultural organizations in the city includes street drama, recitation, music, and discussion meetings. The high level of interest and activities on this day demonstrate the deep attachment and devotion of the Bengalis to their mother tongue.

Twenty-sixth of March is the Independence Day for the nation. On this day in 1971, the people of what is now Bangladesh declared independence following the Pakistani crackdown on an unarmed population. The war of liberation continued until 16th December when the Pakistani forces surrendered to the national army and its allies. Both the occasions are important national events and are duly celebrated every year with colourful processions, military, navy, and air shows, and public rallies.

PRECEDING PAGE (CENTREFOLD)
Under the shade of the great banyan tree in Ramna Park, groups of artists singing Tagore song to celebrate *Pahela Baishakh*, the Bengalee New Year's Day.

TOP AND BOTTOM: Army music band performing open orchestra in Sher-e-Bangla Nagar on the Independence Day celebration on 26 March.

PRECEDING PAGE
TOP AND BOTTOM: Crowds of people gathered in Ramna Park for celebrating the Bengalee New Year's Day.

A Hindu priest offering prayers to goddess Durga
during the observance of Durga Puja in Dhakeswari
Temple.

172

Young girls are dancing inside the Dhakeswari Temple
during Durga Puja celebration.

PRECEDING PAGE
TOP: A religious group discussion in Narinda Hindu Temple.

· BOTTOM: A small sweet shop near Dhakeswari Temple.

TOP: Children in front of a snack shop near the Dhakeswari Temple during the observance of Durga Puja, the biggest religious festival of the Hindu community.

BOTTOM: Pilgrims at the *Biswa Ijtema* in Tongi near Dhaka.

TOP: Gathering of spectators and performers during the opening ceremony of South Asian Federation (SAF) games in the Dhaka stadium in 1994.

BOTTOM: Artists on an open van singing opening chorus during the observance of the South Asian Federation Games in the Dhaka Stadium.

PRECEDING PAGES (CENTREFOLD)
Pilgrims listening to sermon at a lecture session at the *Biswa Ijtema* in Tongi.

FOLLOWING PAGE
Air-dropping of paratroops during the SAF games in the Dhaka stadium.

Pictures in these pages reflect the scenes from the Central Shahid Minar during the observance of the mourning day for the martyrs of the language movement who died on 21st February 1952.

TOP: Scene from an open air drama staged on Shahid Minar premises.

BOTTOM: Floral display of Bangladesh map.

FOLLOWING PAGE
Wreaths are offered at the alter of the Shahid Minar by different organisations including foreign diplomatic missions.

180

Sher-e-Bangla Nagar

10

Sher-e-Bangla Nagar

Sher-e-Bangla Nagar, designed by the famous American architect Louis Kahn in 1965, is often described as a township built with the "rhythm of bricks." The whole schematic plan pivots around the gigantic, octagonal concrete block of the nine-storeyed National Assembly building facing an open plaza on the south. In 1959, the then President General Mohammad Ayub Khan of Pakistan decided in a conference of the Governors to establish a second capital for East Pakistan in Dhaka. Accordingly, in 1951, about 208 acres of land were acquired, north of the present Manik Mia Avenue. Louis Kahn was commissioned to design the masterplan of the Second Capital in 1962.

Its construction was started in 1964-1965 with an initial estimated cost of Rs. 48.6 million and completed with all services and facilities in 1983 at a total revised cost of Tk. 1,332 million (US$ 32 million).

The complex includes the National Assembly Building, Hostels for the Members of the Parliament, Ministers, Secretaries, Hospitality Halls, and Community Buildings, all linked with one another by roads and walkways and surrounded by attractive gardens and lakes. In designing the National Assembly building, one of the important considerations was protection from the sun and rain, while admitting free circulation of air. This has been achieved by providing huge geometric openings at the outer facade in the form of triangles, rectangles, full and segmental circles, and flat arches which provide the visual impressions of this majestic edifice. Thus, the conventional method of placing windows in the exterior was substituted, imparting to the composition, a monumental effect, while removing the disadvantages by the provision of core walls with small gaps in between.

The main building complex consists of nine individual blocks, of which eight at its periphery rise to a height of 110 feet, while the octagonal block at the centre shoots up to a height of 155 feet. The building is relieved at 10 feet intervals with continuous parallel bands of white marble. All these nine blocks surrounding the ambulatory, containing functional spaces at different levels, are inter-linked horizontally and vertically with corridors, lifts, stairs, and circulatory areas, in a harmonious blend. The central block at the core, accommodating the Assembly Chamber, has a total capacity of three hundred fifty-four seats for members of the parliament. It rises to a height of one hundred and seventeen feet with a parabolic shell-roof at the top. The entire complex of the National Assembly Building has a floor area of 8,23,000 square feet in the main building, 2,23,000 square feet in the south plaza, and 65,000 square feet in the Presidential Plaza on the north.

The formal entrance through the south plaza gradually rises to twenty feet and six inches height in a broad flight of stairs. The basement accommodates a parking area, offices of the maintenance agencies, and service installations for the main building.

The citadel of the National Assembly building is linked diagonally on the southeast and southwest by artificial lakes so that the edifice appears to rise out of water. This unique citadel, made of grey concrete blocks amid a complex of otherwise red brick buildings, dominates the entire layout with its lofty contrast, height, and imposing mass. The fundamental character of architecture here is monumental and an adaptation of Islamic building art. In that sense it marks a distinct departure from the rest of the modern buildings and is deeply imbued with the age-old tradition of the land, rooted to its climate and geography.

The Sangsad Bhaban (Parliament Building): The main feature that dominates Sher-e-Bangla Nagar is the Sangsad Bhaban. Designed by the famous American architect, Louis Kahn and constructed at a cost 32 million dollars, this splendid nine-storeyed building has a distinctive architectural style characterised by its geometric shape, interior decorations, and reflecting pool of water outside. The entire neighbourhood is characterised by red brick buildings, gardens, and lakes.

TOP: Crescent Lake Road during the monsoon rain.

BOTTOM: Women workers cleaning the pavement along the Crescent Road.

PRECEDING PAGE
Sangsad Bhaban (Parliament House) during a winter morning mist (TOP) and during spring bloom (BOTTOM).

189

TOP AND BOTTOM: Old men and women relaxing and chatting after their morning stroll along the Crescent Lake

Sangsad Bhaban during winter bloom (TOP) and wet
monsoon (BOTTOM).

Sunrise in Sher-e-Bangla Nagar.

TOP: Sunrise in Sher-e-Bangla Nagar in front of the Agricultural Institute.

BOTTOM: Sangsad Bhaban during night illumination on Victory Day.

194

Open premises around the Sangsad Bhaban provide
an ideal place for karate learners.

A man selling drink of yoghurt to morning strollers in
Sher-e-Bangla Nagar.

A girl taking karate lesson in front of the Sangsad
Bhaban.

Suburban
Dhaka

11

Suburban Dhaka

Dhaka is a fast growing city and its boundaries are rapidly sprawling into the adjoining areas in all directions, mostly towards the north. Although a similar expansion in the south has been limited by the position of the Buriganga, yet the recent construction of some bridges across the river has improved communications and opened up opportunities for the city's expansion across the river beyond Zinjira and Nawabgonj areas.

Suburban areas around Dhaka are characterized by an abrupt change of landscape, the view of the high-rise buildings and towers suddenly changing into that of the flat plains disappearing into the distant horizon. Scattered over this vast plain are the villages and crop lands, mostly rice fields, permeated by narrow trails and small roads, often raised above the ground, that provide communication among the villages and connect them with the main highways passing nearby. In the suburban areas organized structures are rarely seen, although in several areas, mills and factories have been developed, particularly in the outlying areas along the Sitalakhya near Narayanganj. Industrial development has also been concentrated in the northern periphery of the city along the major highways in Tongi and Savar.

The physiography of the outlying regions of Dhaka city is considerably influenced by the seasonal flooding of the surrounding rivers including the Buriganga and the Turag on the southwest, and, the Dhaleswari and the Sitalakhya on the northeast. These rivers, along with their many named and un-named tributaries, constitute an important water transport system for the movement of different commodities to and from the city. Many small and large country boats are frequently seen loading and unloading their cargo at the ports along these rivers.

During the monsoon season, the low-lying plains are completely inundated and remain submerged for about a month or more. During the height of the monsoon, a drive to the outskirts of the city will reveal a stunning view of an immense body of water flooding vast areas of land as far as the eye can see. Distant villages appear as tiny islands of houses and trees floating on water and small country boats are seen plying with their colourful sails. It is often hard to believe that after several days, these waters will disappear completely, exposing the submerged land ready for cultivation again. During heavy flooding, including the one that occurred in 1988, water overflowed the river banks and flooded the city areas, causing considerable damage to life and property. To protect the city from the damaging effects of flooding, a huge embankment has been constructed encircling the city on the southeast.

During the dry season, the landscape provides an entirely different view. There is a high level of activities in the fields, especially the manufacturing of bricks and harvesting of winter crops. The soil of the region is specially suitable for making clay bricks which are burnt in large kilns in the open fields. Raw coal or firewood is used for fueling the kilns and their chimneys, often in clusters, are frequently seen discharging clouds of dark smoke causing considerable pollution of the environment.

Most villagers in suburban areas make their livelihood by farming, fishing, and selling unskilled labour. Although the influence of city life is palpable in the culture of the suburban areas, their fundamental life-styles are primarily rustic in nature.

PRECEDING PAGES (CENTREFOLD)
Sunset across the Turag river near Mirpur bridge.

TOP: Lotus pond in Botanical Garden, Mirpur.
BOTTOM: Amazon lily in Baldha Garden.

TOP: White pelicans and wild migratory birds in the lake of Mirpur Zoo.

BOTTOM: Cargo being unloaded from country boats at the *ghat* near Mirpur bridge.

A rural house-wife bringing water in the village of Amin Bazar on the outskirts of Dhaka.

FOLLOWING PAGES (CENTREFOLD)
Children at play in the suburban village of Nandipara.

Scenes from Nandipara (TOP) and Basabo (BOTTOM).

Setting sun on the bank of Buriganga.

Suggested Reading

Ahmed, N. *Mughal Dhaka and Lalbagh Fort.* Dhaka, 1984.

Ahmed, N. *Discover the Monuments of Bangladesh,* Dhaka: UPL, 1984.

Ahmed, S.U. *Urban Problems and Government Policies: A Case Study of Dhaka City, 1810-1830.* In: K. A. Ballhachet and John Harrison, ed., The City in South Asia: Pre-Modern and Modern. SOAS, University of London, England.

Ahmed, S. U. *Dhaka: Past, Present, Future.* The Asiatic Society of Bangladesh, Dhaka, 1991.

Ashfaq, S. M. *Lalbagh Fort: Monuments and Museums,* Karachi, Pakistan, 1970.

Bradley-Birt, F. B. *Romance of an Eastern Capital.* Smith-Elder & Co, London, England, 1906.

Clay, A. L. *Principal Heads of the History and Statistics of Dacca Division.* Calcutta, 1868.

Dani, A. H. *Dhaka: A record of its Changing Fortune.* Dhaka: 1962.

D'Oyly C. *Antiquities of Dacca.* JJ Landseer & Co, George Bell and Sons, London, 1914.

Dwyer, D. J. *People and Housing in Third World Cities.* Longmans, London, 1975.

Gupta, N. K. *Dacca: Old and New.* Dacca, 1940.

Haider, A. *Dhaka: History and Romance in Place Names.* Dhaka: DMC, 1967.

Hasan, S. M. *Dacca: The City of Mosques.* Dacca, 1981.

Hassan, S. M. *Dacca: Gateway of East Pakistan* (hereafter Dacca: Gateway). Dhaka. 1982.

Heber B. *Narrative of a Journey through the Upper Provinces of India,* London, 1928.

Hussain, S. *Echoes from Old Dacca.* Dhaka: 1909.

Hossain, A. *Dhaka Portrait.* AB Publishers, Dhaka, 1992.

Hossain, A. *A Journey through Bangladesh.* Classic Books International. Dhaka, 1988.

Islam, N. *The People of Dhaka.* Centre for Urban Studies, University of Dhaka, Dhaka, 1982.

James, J. R. *Some Aspects of Town and Country Planning in Bangladesh.* Ford Foundation, Dhaka, 1973.

Karim, A. *Dhaka: The Mughal Capital.* Dhaka: Asiatic Society of Pakistan (now Bangladesh). 1964.

Luhani, G. A. K. *Dacca, Past and Present.* Allahabad, 1911.

Mamun, M. *The Memories of Dhaka City* (in Bengali), Dhaka, Pallab Publishers, 1981.

Majid, R. *The CBD in an Eastern Context: A Case Study of Dacca.* Master's Thesis. London School of Economics, London, 1966.

Majumdar, H. *Reminiscences of Dacca.* Calcutta, 1926.

Rahim, M. A. *The History of the University of Dacca.* Dacca, 1980.

Rizvi, S. N. *Bangladesh District Gazetteers, Dacca.* Dacca, 1975.

Rankin, J. T. *The Study of Antiquities in Dacca.* Reprinted from The Dacca Review. April 1920: Bangladesh Catholic Society, Dhaka, 1988.

Siddiqui, S. K., Kadir, R., Alamgir, S., Huq, S. *Social Formation in Dhaka City.* Dhaka: UPL, 1989.

Taifoor, S. M. *Glimpses of Old Dacca.* Dhaka. S. M. Parwez, ca. 1956.

Taylor, J. A. *A Sketch of the Topography and Statistics of Dacca.* Calcutta. 1840.

Taylor, J. *Topography and Statistics of Dacca.* Calcutta: 1840.